John Watson et al.

The clerical life

John Watson et al.

The clerical life

ISBN/EAN: 9783743335875

Manufactured in Europe, USA, Canada, Australia, Japa

Cover: Foto ©Lupo / pixelio.de

Manufactured and distributed by brebook publishing software (www.brebook.com)

John Watson et al.

The clerical life

THE CLERICAL LIFE

A Series of Letters to Ministers

BY

John Watson, D.D.
Prof. Marcus Dods, D.D.
Prin. T. C. Edwards, D.D.
Prof. James Denney, D.D.
T. H. Darlow, M.A.
T. G. Selby.
W. Robertson Nicoll, LL.D.
J. T. Stoddart.

NEW YORK
DODD, MEAD, AND COMPANY
149–151 Fifth Avenue
1898

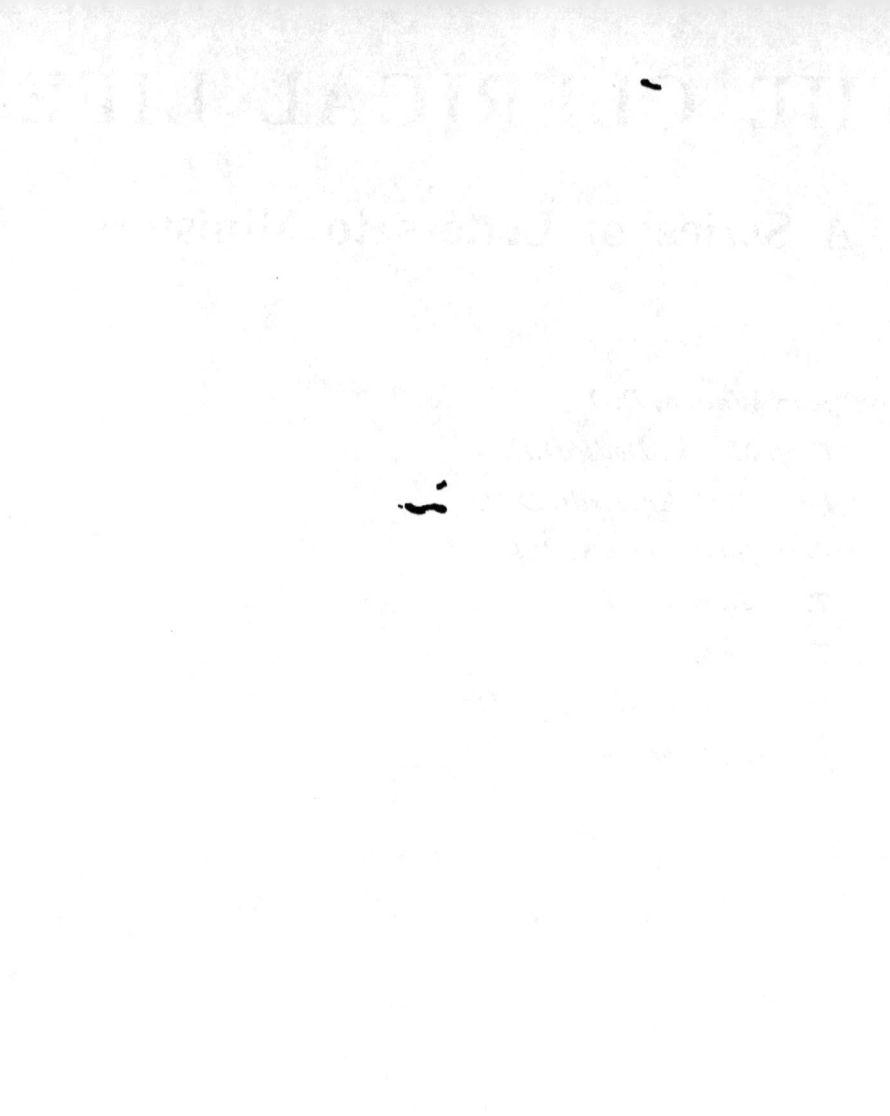

CONTENTS

I
PAGE
TO A MINISTER WHO FINDS THAT SOME OF HIS MOST ATTRACTIVE YOUNG MEN ARE SCEPTICAL, . . 3

II
TO A YOUNG MINISTER WHO IS GIVEN TO ANECDOTAGE IN THE PULPIT, ... 19

III
TO A YOUNG MINISTER WHO HAS BEEN INVITED TO PREACH IN A VACANT CHURCH, . . . 33

IV
TO A MINISTER WHOSE SERMONS LAST AN HOUR, . 43

V

To a Minister who has no Theology in his Sermons, ... 55

VI

To a Minister whose Preaching is a Failure, . 67

VII

To a Minister who is unsuccessful with Children, ... 79

VIII

To a Ministerial Sir Willoughby Patterne, . 93

IX

To a Minister who regards himself as a Prophet of Criticism, ... 105

X

From a Minister who is asked to many Tea-Parties, ... 117

CONTENTS

XI
TO A YOUNG MINISTER WHO REFUSED TO WEAR A WHITE TIE, ... 129

XII
TO A MINISTER WHO BECOMES PERIODICALLY 'RUN DOWN,' 139

XIII
TO A MINISTER TROUBLED BY INTELLECTUAL DISPARITIES IN HIS CONGREGATION, ... 151

XIV
TO A MINISTER WHO HAS STUDIED IN GERMANY, . 167

XV
TO A DIVINITY STUDENT, ... 179

XVI
TO A MARTYR OF PROCRASTINATING AND PESSIMISTIC MOODS IN SERMONISING, . . . 191

XVII

TO A MINISTER WHO OBJECTS TO 'WANDERING' IN AUGUST, ... 211

XVIII

TO A BROTHER SMARTING UNDER A BAD TIME, . . 223

XIX

TO A MINISTER WHO HAS WARNED HIS PEOPLE AGAINST 'INTELLECTUAL PREACHING,' 235

XX

TO A MINISTER WHO INCLINES TO CONDESCENSION, . 247

I

To a Minister who finds that some of his most attractive Young Men are Sceptical

A

To a Minister who finds that some of his most attractive Young Men are Sceptical

My dear X.,—You tell me in your last interesting letter, what I am by no means surprised to learn, that some of the finest, most companionable, and most serviceable young men in your congregation are sceptical. Yours is not an unprecedented experience. In an age in which everything is called in question, and each man has to find his own way to his own measure of faith, it is not surprising that many intelligent and earnest minds should spend some considerable time in hesitation, doubt, and questioning. The wonder rather is that so many find a resting-place on *terra firma*. It is a *sauve qui peut*, as in Paul's shipwreck, 'some on boards and some on broken pieces of the old ship'; the marvel still being that so many escape 'safe to land.' Scepticism is the price we have to pay for the advances we are making in knowledge. It results from the difficulty of reconciling the new truth with the old. It is one element in the 'growing pains' of the world. It is inevitable, and in one aspect both satisfactory and hopeful.

Scepticism exists in so many different forms and strengths, it has such a variety of phases and stages, and it arises from causes so diverse, that it is impossible to recommend a treatment which will be universally applicable and effective. That eminent specialist in scepticism, the Rev. A. J. Harrison, divides unbelievers into no fewer than ten classes, according as their mental attitude is identified with Indifference, Naturalism, Doubt, Antipathy, Atheism, Pantheism, Deism, Agnosticism, Positivism, or Secularism. Such lists are somewhat appalling, as they present to the mind a more definite conception of the magnitude of the evil, and as we recognise that even in small and ordinary congregations specimens of these various types are to be found in a more or less developed form, you will not, I feel sure, expect me to enter into a detailed description of the treatment which each special case demands, but will be satisfied if I merely set down some general principles applicable to all

When confronted with actual instances of scepticism, we at once perceive that some of them are rather due to moral causes, while others have their root in mental perplexity or mere ignorance. The former are the most baffling and the most trying to the temper: incurable save by a moral revolution. If a man flaunts his unbelief, and is glad to find a pretext for prolonging it, what he needs is that enlargement of view and that deepening of nature which come with a sense of sin. A broken heart is the pre-requisite for any fruitful consideration of spiritual truth. This we must aim at producing by our preaching, but only God's providence and Spirit can accomplish the needful change. Similarly it is only the hand of God in the life and spirit of the individual which can scatter the gloom which through untoward and distressing calamity has settled on the entire outlook and rendered everything dim and uncertain. It is in such circumstances that a minister reaps the benefit of having gained the confidence of his people, and of having lived on terms of frank intimacy with them. For apart from previous friendship it is difficult to find access to a bruised and embittered spirit; whereas, if it has become natural to speak frankly, a word boldly spoken in season may be the turning-point in a soul's history.

And in cases where the scepticism is the result rather of mental than of moral causes, friendliness is still the prime requisite in a minister—not a professed or professional, but a real and hearty interest in the questionings of the perplexed. This friendliness not only makes your resources available for the doubter, but it is itself a material encouragement and aid to him. In your faith he has a reminder of the possibility of believing, and this unconsciously breeds hope in him. Your sympathy preserves him from counting himself an outcast from the Church, and so saves him from becoming soured and reckless. To utter our doubts and definitely place them before another mind is often a long step towards their dismissal. Faith, moreover, is a more contagious quality than we sometimes imagine; and at all times it is well to remember the maxim: Exemplo plus quam ratione vivimus; a maxim which is true even of those who deny and denounce its possible application to themselves.

If you are to be as helpful to the sceptical as you desire, you must determine with some precision what are the necessary contents of the Christian creed. On a liberal interpretation of Christian faith, is this or that man, after all, a sceptic? Sceptical of some things which others believe, we must all always be. Certain knowledge regarding all Divine truth is impossible. And we may be in the unhappy position of demanding so much faith as to repel men from Christianity, even while we seek to recommend it to them. Where is the line to be drawn between the scepticism that is inevitable and the scepticism that is detrimental and unchristian? Much may, I think, be learned from our Lord's method. He, by the nature of the case, was required to deal with men at every stage of belief or unbelief. And the inexorable, explicit and exacting demands He made upon men ethically are not more remarkable than the narrow limits within which He required acceptance of theological propositions. He was abundantly satisfied when Peter and the rest had been led on to the conviction that He was the Christ, and on this article of the creed He founded His Church. It is by adherence to that confession that the gates of hell are rendered powerless. This simplicity of creed is thrown into the most striking relief by the absolute character of the demands made on the personal devotedness of His followers. The ministers of Christ must follow Him in insisting that the same relation be maintained between the claims of Christ on the personal attachment and obedience of men, and all demands on their mental acknowledgment of propositions regarding Him and His work. The minister of Christ has no right to replace stumbling-blocks which He Himself was careful to remove. He has no right to make the entrance into the kingdom straiter than Christ made it. The question being, not how to perfect, but how to win disciples, it is unwise and it is unlawful to demand belief in Inspiration, or in a definite theory of the Atonement, or in other doctrines which are sometimes reckoned essentials.

If these doctrines are true and helpful to the Christian life, then the disciple will find them out, but to demand acceptance of them at the gate is to drive honest and self-knowing men away. Does a man accept Jesus as the Christ? This is the Apostolic test. Does a man see in Jesus the representative of God on earth and the true head and Redeemer of men, and does he personally own this leadership? Then he is a Christian of the New Testament type. His faith is radical, his scepticism superficial.

In thus dealing with supposed sceptics, you must be prepared to be misunderstood and to be misrepresented. The most notable attempt in our time to reconcile Christian faith with advancing science was branded as itself destructive of the faith. When Mr. Gore and his associates strove to make the entrance to the kingdom wide enough to admit men of science, and issued *Lux Mundi* with the intention of showing that truth is one and Christian, Archdeacon Denison characterised the book as 'the most grievous specimen of defence of truth of all those I have had to contend against, and the most ruinous under all the circumstances of its production, a blow *ab intra* without parallel.' So it is always. To reach a helping hand to the sceptical is commonly understood to be treachery. Eating with publicans and sinners is in some forms of it still condemned by many orthodox people. In some critical times almost in the same proportion as you give your sympathy and help to the sceptical must you lose the respect of Christian people and endure the suspicion and coldness of former friends. You must therefore count the cost of seeking truth for yourself and carrying to those in darkness the light you have yourself found. 'All things on earth have their price; and for truth we pay the dearest. We barter it for love and sympathy. The road to honour is paved with thorns ; but on the path to truth, at every step you set your foot down on your own heart.'

You must also be prepared for disappointment. Arguments which to you seem conclusive produce no result. Suggestions which have brought relief to your mind take no root in the mind of another. And yet it is beyond question that much may be accomplished by judicious counsel, whether in the pulpit or in private. In an interesting letter to the late Dean Stanley, Mr. J. R. Green, the historian, tells him that in his lecture-room he was saved from scepticism. He had gone up to Oxford a hard reader and a pronounced and enthusiastic High Churchman. But two years' residence found him idle and irreligious. 'High Churchism fell with a great crash, and left nothing behind—nothing but a vague reverence for goodness.' It was the wise and kindly liberalism of Stanley which built up for him once more a Christian faith. And when Renan tells us that with his belief in the inspiration and infallibility of every word of the Old Testament he felt constrained to throw overboard the whole orthodox creed, we cannot read his naïve confessions without being amazed that a man of his acuteness and knowledge should so confound the essentials with the accidents of Christianity, and without wishing that there had been at his elbow a judicious friend who had already thought his way through these morning mists. No doubt controversial discussion is apt to generate more heat than light. But friendly and natural talk about the subjects of greatest interest to earnest men at the very least prevents scepticism from hardening into dogmatic unbelief, and may in the most unexpected manner prove of critical importance.

Conversation of this kind will of course guide itself; but it is especially needful to urge upon the sceptical the need of personal and first-hand knowledge. The ignorance of Christianity which is manifested even by leading Agnostics is amazing and perplexing. And the simplicity with which many persons accept the crude statements made in popular literature is the chief source of danger. The representative of Christianity must if possible hit the mean between turning a deaf ear to science and credulously accepting as proved every assertion of any scientific man. He must inculcate and himself exemplify the patient prudence which is prepared to give a cordial welcome to all truth, but which can wait until suppositions and inferences and speculations are either proved or disproved. To accept everything which at present is advanced under the name of Biblical Criticism is as prejudiced and unwise and perhaps as dangerous as to condemn all criticism and repudiate all its conclusions. It is part of the ministerial function to sift truth from error in the results of modern investigation, and, without annoying and perplexing the bulk of the people who have little interest in such matters, to aid the lay mind in distinguishing between what is proved and what is as yet merely conjectured.

With a certain small class of minds something may be accomplished by recommending relevant reading. One never can forget the experience of the late George Bowen, one of the most remarkable and original, as he was certainly one of the most convinced Christians of the century. By a singular accident Paley's *Evidences* came into his hands. 'He would not read it; he knew all about the evidences of Christianity; he had long ago finally settled that question. Before putting it away, however, he glanced at the first sentence, and was arrested by it. He read one page, and another, and another; was pleased with the style and the candour of the writer, and at last sat down and read a good portion of the book. To his surprise he found he was beginning to take a new view of the evidences, and then shut up the book, and put it aside, afraid of being surprised into any change of belief.' The book ultimately prevailed. Perhaps those who have fought their own way to a believing position are apt to underrate the influence of books. They remember how irritated they themselves were by inadequate explanations, inept reflections, irrelevant argument. Still, it is unquestionable that studious and candid minds find in books a more complete solution of current difficulties than they can expect either in conversation or in sermons. Fisher, Newman, Smyth, Wace, Harrison, Row, and others have treated various parts of the evidences in a manner which cannot but appeal to those who are really seeking truth.

At present a peculiar phase of scepticism prevails, which perhaps deserves a word to itself. Among the working classes there seems to be a growing resentment against the Church for its supposed or real non-interference in labour disputes. Christianity is being judged by its power to lighten the burden and right the wrongs of the oppressed; and in many instances it is being rejected as helpless for present needs, promising much but performing little. This is precisely the scepticism of John the Baptist. He lay in his dungeon listening for the crash of revolution and the shout of the armed followers of the Messiah sweeping oppression from the land, and all he heard was the indistinct rumour of a few sick healed and one or two old blind beggars restored. He could not understand why nothing decisive was immediately accomplished. He began to doubt whether indeed Jesus could after all be the Messiah. John had to learn, and many in our own day have to learn, that the method of Jesus is not superficial, but radical; that it begins at the beginning of all evil and slowly works its way to results that are permanent. To one who demanded the interference of Jesus He replied, 'Who made me a Judge over you?' But at the same time He lodged such principles in human society as produce justice and charity. He does not strive nor cry, He does not rule by spasmodic interference or measures of violence. His methods are inward, spiritual, and gradual, and, 'Blessed is he whosoever is not offended in Him.'—Yours, etc., ZETA.

II

To a Young Minister who is given to Anecdotage in the Pulpit

To a Young Minister who is given to Anecdotage in the Pulpit

DEAR DRYVELL,—It was a happy touch of Lord Beaconsfield to describe an elderly man as in his anecdotage, but it struck me when I had the pleasure of hearing you preach last Sunday that you had arrived at this stage somewhat prematurely and not very successfully.

Your sermon was less than forty minutes, and within that space you included six anecdotes, given with lavish conversational detail, and you also displayed a wealth of anecdotal allusion which inferred on the part of your hearers a flattering remembrance of past sermons and a minute acquaintance with the more flamboyant religious literature of our day. References to your remarkable experiences in evangelistic work would lead any one, unacquainted with the generous use of language characteristic of your school, to believe either that you were fifty years old, or that you had begun to labour for the spiritual good of your fellow-creatures at the early age of five. Perhaps one may not be far out in the calculation that you are about twenty-eight, in which case your attached people have some cause for anxiety as they anticipate the future, when you are, say, sixty, and begin to look at them from above your spectacles. It comes to the rule of three, and although I judge that your training in mathematics has not been severe, this is an easy application. If your preaching be in the proportion of fifty per cent. of fluid to fifty per cent. of solid when you have hardly left college and the habit of study must still have some hold, what will it be when you have ceased to assimilate new ideas and the sinews of the mind are relaxed? It works out five per cent. of instruction floating in ninety-five per cent. of fiction, and suggests the condition of those public schools, if you will pardon an alien illustration, where the legend runs that the boys have a break of five minutes every hour for Latin.

Very likely you will harden yourself against

this well-intended remonstrance with the reflection that its writer is a superior person who sniffs at a popularity he has never been able to obtain, and with the evident fact that you have filled your church. It was only yesterday that an expansive father congratulated you because he had no difficulty now in bringing his young people to service, and the only complaint at the supper table was the shortness of the sermon. 'You give it us tasty,' something like that were his words, 'and the public demands flavour nowadays.' You winced for the moment under the form of the worthy man's eulogy, but you had some just pride last Sunday in his well-filled pew. It happened that a family of this kind sat before me, and there is no doubt they were deeply interested, the father leaning forward and smiling up the pew at your racier sallies, while a daughter underlined your points with nudges. You lost them once in the interval between the anecdotes —when the son yawned almost audibly, and the girls compared notes by code on a neighbouring bonnet—but you had them well in hand with that vivacious proposal scene. It gave a quiet man pause, but it was certainly memorable, and one was glad that your impossible application to personal religion was quite obscured by the spray of merriment. One was a little concerned by the contemptuous look on a young man's face—clever face too, Herbert Spencer man, I should say; and the sigh of an old saint near me—leaves of his Bible worn thin at the Psalms and St. John's Gospel—would have made you sad. No one looked at the clock, but the people who never think of a clock went empty away.

You ought, however, to be congratulated on the reserves of your anecdotage, which were most grateful to one at least of your audience. No call was made on the saint—Baxter or Newton in England, Rutherford or Chalmers in Scotland —who saw a murderer going to his doom, and said: 'Had it not been for grace, there goes [fill in];' or on the dramatic English Consul, who wrapped the Union Jack round an afflicted countryman and dared the native authorities to fire; or the French soldier who whispered to the surgeon: 'An inch farther, and you touch the Emperor;' or the conscript who bought a substitute, and objected very properly to be called again—who have long made tableaux vivants for the illustration of various doctrines. It is pleasant to know that, in your opinion, these war-worn veterans should be released from active service, and sent into a well-earned rest.

One does not, of course, mean that the infallible criterion of an anecdote is its newness; for, indeed, it is very often its oldness. Anecdotes and wines have this likeness, that the thinnest must be taken in their youth, for they will not last; but the richest are grateful to the palate in their mature age. Plutarch's *Lives* contain a lode which the pulpit has never worked, although there is plenty of gold among the quartz. The mystics had the most lovely parables. The 'ages of Faith' have left us legends which are perfect sermons, the fragrant essence of fields of flowers. Ancient martyrology, the lives of chief saints, the select annals of the Foreign Mission crusade, lie to a man's hand. Stories gathered from such quarters have in them a certain distinction that defies ridicule and refuses to be vulgarised. No theme is too august for their introduction, no class is either so cultured or so simple that it will refuse them hearing. One or two exceptions may be made; for even the Sistine Madonna becomes a weariness when thrust upon your eyes from every print-shop, not because of antiquity, but because of repetition. It may be taken for granted that your hearers are painfully familiar with the age of the martyr Polycarp, and that the derivation of Christopher has been finally lodged in the mind of the religious public. But, after all deductions, the riches are immense. Perhaps, to take only two instances at random, because they happened to have been finely handled by Whittier, your people have not heard of the 'Gift of Tritemius' or the story of 'Barclay of Ury.' It is only possible to indicate the outer door of this treasure-house, but I am tempted to add that many a commonplace sermon might be perfumed, as if it had been kept in a sandal-wood box, by the 'Fiorretti di San Francesco.'

Preachers of your school are at a double disadvantage in the use of contemporary anecdotage. The most acceptable anecdotes have not sprung full-grown from life, but from some artist's brain.

Some friend, with confidence in this man's powers, has brought him the raw material, which is usually either American or Scotch—in a few very grateful cases French—and this expert weaves the confused mass into a piquant pattern, each point of colour and shape having been carefully considered. The finished product is admirable in an after-dinner speech, or in the causerie of a monthly—it might even be introduced into a political or ecclesiastical speech, although the experiment would be risky, as those audiences have a fruity palate—but it is manifestly unfit for the pulpit. Possibly its subject might be religion —the two best anecdotes of the last six months have been profoundly religious. The style is, however, an insuperable objection to such anecdotes. They are works of art.

Your anecdotes are free from this charge, but they have no corresponding compensation. One has no conviction that they are true. It is not merely that you laid the scene of one of your most moving tales in the East End of London, while the 'Scottish Chrysostom' gave it two weeks ago as his own experience in the Canongate of Edinburgh, or that you yourself varied the hero's name from John to James within five minutes. One discrepancy might be really a coincidence, the other a slip of the tongue. What blights religious anecdotage and makes it an offence is its apparent unreality. Nine men out of ten, at the lowest, believe it an absolute invention—and very poor at that—and they can find internal evidence for their faith. An anecdote may pass as art without being true (in the witness-box sense) or as truth without being art (in the picture-gallery sense); but what if there be neither art nor truth?

Let me assure you at once that I do not bring any charge of personal falsehood, for the thought of your school is so out of touch with reality that accuracy in the relation of facts has become impossible. When you gave that shock to your fellow-passenger in the express by informing him that he was not on the way to London, and then so worked upon him with your spiritual-railroad parable that he could only hold your hand at Euston, you laid a burden upon us heavier than we could bear. I was not there, but one has some slight knowledge of human nature, and if you had played that wrong-train trick on any man I know, when the train was going eighty (?) miles an hour, he had only stopped short of an assault, and he would not have been one whit conciliated by your intrusion into his most sacred affairs. Besides, are you certain that 'the tears were streaming down his cheeks' as you parted, and does every person say 'Sir' in addressing you upon such occasions? Are these inevitable 'tears' and this endless refrain of 'Sir' the phenomena of genuine religion?

'Sir' came in some eight times in that conversation, always to you, but another word rose to fourteen. It was 'I,' and that leads me to suggest that if you feel obliged to illustrate the Gospel by the records of your family history, you might practise devices. Why not say 'one' instead of 'I,' and 'a mother once said to her son,' instead of 'my mother was a plain woman, and I'm not ashamed of it, and she said'? Perhaps it was some feeling of this sort made you conduct dialogues with yourself as 'David Dryvell,' but this stroke was less than felicitous. It is good to have one's message soaked in life, but humanity is wider than one's relatives. The man who has seen most of life says least about his family, and the miscreant who will utilise his mother's death-bed in a sermon ought to be deposed from the Christian ministry.

You did not commit that impiety; but it remains a grave question whether the public are specially interested in a preacher's family annals. If your father had been a marquis you would have considered it bad taste to introduce him, and it is not any better because, as you assured us, he belonged to the proletariat. What gives, however, your father some claim on the public is his amazing versatility. You once described his eviction from a little farm with such pathos that it was mentioned in the *Daily Scorpion*. At the great meeting of railway servants you described his dangers as the brakesman of a goods train. When there was trouble among the dockers we were given to understand he had shared their hard lot, and if the miners go out on strike I am morally certain that your father will have been killed in an explosion. It is possible that he was all those things in turn, but it is not likely; and one is haunted with the suspicion that he was none of them, but that least picturesque and yet very useful member of the community—the *bête noire* of the proletariat—a small tradesman.

This letter is written with much frankness, and may not be agreeable, but I wish you to believe that it is sincere and also consistent with respect. Let me acknowledge your conspicuous excellencies and the pledges you have given to success. You are not a pedant droning out college essays, nor a superior person relying on the approbation of a select circle, nor a cheap iconoclast attacking the theology you do not understand, nor a selfish professionalist greedy of gain. Your sympathy with humanity is genuine, and your enthusiasm for the Kingdom of God is admirable. Your virtues are your own, your vices are those of your school. One would like to see your sympathy banked up that it may run in a deeper channel, and your enthusiasm severely pruned that it may bear richer fruit.

When you have read this letter you will be angry with me and count me a scorner, but I shall be sustained by one solid satisfaction. As you are under thirty years of age and are not yet intoxicated with spiritual pride, you will never again fall into those follies I have tried to describe. LAMBDA.

III

*To a Young Minister who has been invited
to Preach in a vacant Church*

To a Young Minister who has been Invited to Preach in a Vacant Church

MY DEAR SIR,—You have been three years in your present charge in the Highlands of Scotland. During that time, you tell me, you have had no great trouble or failure, and no marked success. You have been invited to preach in a city church, the minister of which died lately, and you ask me whether you should do so.

My answer is meant to be brief and practical, but it is impossible to treat anything in the life of a true minister from the secular point of view. I cannot but sympathise with your desire to be in the full swing of an active career. There are hours when everything around you seems puny and diminutive. You could hardly live through them if it were not for the hope of livelier and more golden times. It is part of the loving plan of God that the possibilities in life are all but unbounded, that there may be at any time a miraculous turn of the wheel. A margin of the indefinable is necessary for our peace. What you do not know, what you probably will not believe, is that it is as necessary to those who have attained the goal you aim at as it is for you. If you ask the men in the ministry who have obtained most of what is called prominence and success, they could tell you that they, too, have a sense of something unsatisfying, something unattained in their careers, a feeling which they keep secret, but which is painful enough in its quiet way. God is not ashamed to be called their God, seeing He has prepared for them a city. To the last they have their hidden dreams, and it is best that we should go on dreaming till the filmy curtains are parted, and we reach that reality in which all dreams merge and end.

Nor is there anything contemptible in the desire to win acceptance with the multitude. 'He was not what in these days is called a popular preacher, let us thank God!' were the words of Baldwin Brown when one of his friends died. There is a popularity to be loathed and feared—

THE CLERICAL LIFE

the popularity of those who stand by the solemn abyss of truth, burning blue lights over it, and throwing yelping crackers into it. But you will never aim at that, and you will never, I believe, deserve such verses as one of George Macdonald's characters composed about his minister:

> ''Twas a sair, sair day, 'twas my hap till
> Come under yer soon ! Mr. Sclater ;
> But things maun be putten a stap till,
> An' sae maun ye, seener or later !
>
> For to hear ye rowtin' an' scornin'
> Is no' to hark to the river ;
> An' to sit here till brak trowth's mornin'
> Wad be to be lost for ever.'

But the power of using the gift of speech for the good of your fellows is a sacred and precious trust. If the common people heard Christ gladly, popularity need be no reproach to any preacher.

At the same time I do not hesitate in advising you to decline the invitation. For one thing, you will probably not succeed. It is likely, as things are managed in these days, that the congregation has heard other preachers. The members, or a large number of them, may be satisfied with one who has already appeared in their pulpit. In that case you cannot hope to change their minds. It is very likely that you will not do yourself justice unless you are perfectly convinced that you are doing what is right and honourable and wise. Some disturbing element will invade your peace and destroy your self-command. Other preachers may be following you, and any impression you make may be soon effaced. I am discussing the matter on the lowest grounds, because if you knew that you would not be called to the church, you would not have had the slightest occasion to write me. Well, suppose you fail and go back to your people, it is possible they may not discover what you have done, although this is not at all likely. Even if they do not, there is a secret henceforth between them and you, a little rift within the lute. If they know, their relation towards you is more or less altered. What romance in it remained has practically disappeared. You will also be unsettled as you wait for the result and think of other vacancies where you may succeed if you fail in this. There is nothing which more surely poisons a minister's heart and life than thought and speech of that kind. It is a poor thing to say that, looking at the matter from the commercial point of view, you have cheapened yourself, but it is true. In ninety-nine cases out of a hundred, ministers who preach in vacancies live to regret it bitterly.

If you had been many years in your parish, if your domestic circumstances were different, if you felt that your work in the place was done, then the question would be less easy to answer. After all, we must take things as we find them, and as such matters are arranged in the churches, there may be but one way of securing a needed change. In that case it would be best to speak frankly to the leading men in your congregation. A minister who has done good work for a term of years may, as a rule, depend on their taking a considerate view of his position. I own that sometimes that may be impossible. It may be for a man's self-respect and peace that he should resign, even though by resigning he may make it much more difficult to secure another pastorate. In any case we must remember that no minister can lightly fall below his own sense of what is honourable, decent, upright, self-respecting.

How happy are those ministers who believe in youth what most of us have to be taught through innumerable blunders and heart-breaking humiliations, happy if even so we come to know it! All our thought at first is that we can order life, that if we devise and plan and labour we will in due time find our legitimate place and true sphere of work. We find it hard to believe that God does not forget His faithful servants for all the ups and downs of the hills. At last we discover that we cannot order life, that it comes flowing on us from behind, that our duty, as a great teacher has said, is to fall in with the forces at work, to do every moment's labour aright, and then let come —not what will, for there is no such thing—but what the eternal thought meant for each one of us. How much more worthy, serene, wise our days would have been if from their fresh morning they had been filled with that faith. But only by slow unveilings did the truth grow clear, and so our salvation tarried.

If it is your lot to end your days where you are,

do not fancy that you are without the means of truest happiness. How many whose lot has been cast later in places more exacting and clamorous, look back with yearning affection to the heather, the hills, and the burns. Was there never a time when the poor little kirk—often mist-soaked or snow-locked—was transfigured to you—' never an hour—say of moaning midnight—when the kirk hung spectral in the sky, and Being was, as it were, swallowed up of Darkness'? But your work is with humanity—with the redemption o humanity. Consider the burdens of your people, and you will forget your own. We ask too much of life; are importunate in craving for a happiness denied to others, and to which we have no right. Learn to sympathise with your neighbours, to penetrate beneath the outward mask which words throw over thought, to read their very hearts. Remember that you and they are sharers in the life of the wonderful Church of Christ. No two maxims should be more with the minister than these—*Homo sum nihil humani a me alienum puto*, and 'The whole creation groaneth and travaileth in pain together until now.'—Yours sincerely,

OMEGA.

IV

To a Minister whose Sermons last an Hour

To a Minister whose Sermons last an Hour

DEAR MR. LONGWYNDE,—When you surveyed our church from the platform on the evening of your recognition meeting, you whispered in my ear that you wished the clock could be removed. The newest and handsomest churches, you reminded me, have no clocks. At the moment I could not imagine why you had taken a dislike to our friendly old timepiece, which had ticked on peacefully during your predecessor's reign. Now, alas! many members of the congregation seem to wish that the clock would serve you as the bell did the lazy scholar in Goethe's ballad —lay violent hands upon you and bring your sermons to a close. I myself have no sympathy with these complaints. I like long sermons, and if all your hearers had my patience, you would never need to apologise for the length of your preaching. Your list of excuses would make a sermon in itself. There is first the importance of the subject, next the copiousness of matter, thirdly the need of repetition and expansion in dealing with a London congregation. You will forgive me if I repeat quite frankly what the grumblers say on these points.

They admit the importance of reverent and unhurried public worship, but they complain that the early parts of the service are shortened to make room for the sermon. The younger people are angry because they are seldom allowed to sing more than three verses of a hymn. 'Hymn 98, verses first and last,' is, they say, your favourite formula. This request for more singing seems to me unreasonable, partly, perhaps, because neither I nor any of my children has an ear for music. The reading of Scripture occupies three minutes, and the prayers five minutes each. On the other hand, there is never any hurry over the collection, and we have the pleasure each Sunday of hearing a fresh exhortation to liberality. Sometimes, too, you give us most interesting comments on the Scripture lesson. When I

THE CLERICAL LIFE

hear that 'a number of striking and profitable reflections' have occurred to you on the Psalm just read, I make up my mind with satisfaction that the service will last two hours. The grumblers ask why your watch lies on the desk before you during the first twenty minutes, and reposes in your pocket during the sermon?

As for the second point, no one ventures to dispute your gifts of eloquence, or the riches and variety of your mental equipment. What you lack, it is said, is the power of selection. The subjects you prefer are those which range over a wide area of the Bible. 'The History of Balaam,' 'The Disobedience and Punishment of Jonah,' furnished you with instructive morning sermons. To my mind, these discourses were full of subtle analysis and of marvellous description. I shall never forget the word-picture you drew of Balaam looking down from the mountains upon the tents of Israel. Other members say, however, that your sermons on Scripture characters are little more than a running commentary. The truth is, they do not like the trouble of using their Bibles in church. You are rightly severe on the modern practice of coming to church provided simply with a hymn-book. Few things add more to the attraction of your preaching than your custom of tracking names and places from one end of the Bible to the other. 'It will be a profitable exercise, brethren,' you said last Sunday, 'to see what is told us about Esau in the New Testament. Turn with me, first of all, to the Epistle to the Hebrews.' I had been getting a little drowsy, as one does after a hard week in the City, but by the time I had found the verse in my own Bible and in those of my four children, I felt thoroughly revived. I like your practice of taking a single verse, and showing how the whole of Scripture can be made to bear upon it. Some weeks ago you preached from the words, 'Then shall every man have praise of God.' Beginning with Abel, and gradually working through Old Testament history, you drew up a list of praiseworthy actions. Next you reviewed the heroic deeds recorded in the New Testament, and as people were beginning by that time to slip out by the door farthest away from the pulpit, you announced that a fuller exegesis of the passage would be reserved for the evening. I returned in the evening full of interest and expectancy, and was astonished to find so small a congregation.

Among the charms of your sermons is their wealth of quotation and anecdote. My wife believes that you have learned by heart nearly the whole of English poetry. My eldest son points out that your extracts are invariably taken from the 'Thousand and One Gems,' but, even if he is right, immense labour would be required to commit them to memory. Longfellow, who appears to be your favourite poet, is mine and my wife's as well, and we never hear a verse from 'The Psalm of Life' without a thrill of satisfaction. We like your habit of repeating the same anecdote in different sermons. This helps to stamp the lesson on the memory, and it must be a poor tale that will not bear retelling. Yet people complain of your extracts and your stories. Only last Wednesday one of the deacons said we might suppose, from your anecdotes about the Royal Family, that the Queen is constantly engaged in presenting Bibles to savage chieftains.

It is a singular proof of the bad taste of our part of London, that objection should be taken to the personal references in your sermons. 'I hope no one will think me egotistical,' you remarked on a recent occasion. 'No man is more free from self-love, or the desire for self-glorification. The truth is, we all know much about ourselves, and next to nothing about other people; therefore personal experiences are the only experiences worth telling.' Many complained because, on Harvest Sunday, when the text was, 'Seed-time and harvest shall not cease,' the greater part of the sermon was taken up with an account of your holiday at Eastbourne. My wife and I were prevented from leaving London last summer, and we enjoyed hearing about your walks on Beachy Head. It is the personal element in your preaching which draws crowds to the church.

You are quite right in thinking that repetition is necessary in sermons meant for London congregations. There is, unfortunately, a growing tendency to drowsiness among our members. I cannot conceive what the cause of this may be, although I frankly admit I drop off to sleep much oftener than in the time of our former minister. Advancing years may be a sufficient explanation in my case, and it is pleasant to know, if I should chance for a few moments to be overcome with heaviness, that when I wake you will be presenting the same truth under a slightly varied aspect. I sometimes think our church is overheated, for even the younger hearers show a marked inclination to somnolence. We are fortunate in having a pastor who will bear with our infirmities, reiterating his arguments until even the dullest brain can grasp his meaning.

It is a singular circumstance that so many of the pewholders are moving away from the seats around the pulpit, and are taking sittings near the door. One explanation may be that they kindly wish to leave the best places for strangers. I have heard it whispered that many prefer pews from which they can retire unnoticed if the sermon exceeds the usual length. For my own part, I like to sit with my family well in view of the pulpit, and to set an example of regular and punctual attendance.

Nothing proves more strikingly your great skill

as a preacher than the apologies you have ready as the sermon proceeds. As there are no divisions, we are carried smoothly and pleasantly on, without any severe tax on the memory. When the subject is fairly opened up, and a few of the younger and more impatient hearers are beginning to fidget with their hymn-books, you cleverly introduce some phrase which proves that the end is in sight. 'Now, brethren, the remaining points may be very briefly considered'; 'Not to fatigue the attention of the congregation, let me pass on at once to the closing scenes of Balaam's history'; 'Time would fail to exhaust the wealth of this passage, so let me in closing throw out a few practical lessons from the subject.' These 'few practical lessons' make a sermon in themselves. They have a 'First of all,' a 'further, brethren,' a 'finally,' an 'in conclusion,' and a 'last of all.' I am never weary of admiring the versatility of intellect which enables you to see so many lessons in a single text.

People complain that your preaching is not memorable, but that is because they will not take notes. I filled six large note-books during last winter, and if you should wish to publish a volume, you will find the substance of your discourses in my possession. It is odd that publishers do not recognise their saleable qualities. When I leave my note-book at home I remember little, but this is not surprising in a man who has passed his fiftieth birthday. My elder children repeat your most interesting anecdotes at the tea-table. My younger children are not now allowed to come to church, although under our late minister they came every morning. My wife's invalid sister has also given up church-going, because she finds the long sermons so exhausting. She is teasing me at present to take the back pew in the gallery.

Your severest critics must confess that you never preach old sermons. In this you present an admirable contrast to many ministers whose reputation stands high. Professor Woodcroft, for instance, is a great man, but I hear he has only six sermons, each of which he has delivered at least fifty times. Depend upon it that, when your brother ministers complain of your verbosity, they are meanly envious of your genius.

An attempt is to be made, I hear, to induce you to shorten your sermons, but you may be trusted to resist such tyranny. I warned the deacons, at their last meeting, that you were not a man to be driven. I had also the pleasure of telling them that, whoever might grumble, you had the grateful appreciation and sympathy of one at least of your members. X.

V

To a Minister who has no Theology in his Sermons

To a Minister who has no Theology in his Sermons

MY DEAR C.,—I know you have strong convictions, or at least that you use strong language, about what you call theological preaching, but I have heard you once or twice lately, and venture to brave your indignation for what I will call your good. If you were a careless fellow, who preached without preparation and without soul, I should not think of writing you in this strain; and it is only because I seem to see plainly how you could make your work much more effective that I presume to act the critic.

You frankly avow your dislike of the theological sermon. I have heard you rail many a time at the formalism, the pedantry, the lifelessness of definitions, and expatiate on the interest and attractiveness of life. You accept without any drawback the contrast of literature and dogma, and you are even more dogmatic than Matthew Arnold, in the assurance with which you put the Old and New Testaments under your favourite heading, and exclude them from the other. You scorn the proof-text theory of Scripture, which makes it a quarry for the dogmatist to slave in, instead of a park where any gentleman may walk abroad. You dread giving your young people a distaste for the truth of God by doing it up into any kind of pemmican, however pure and nutritious it may be. You prefer to show them the range of the pasture, to pluck flowers for them here and there, to make what is human and incidental in it vivid, to be ethical, imaginative, practical—anything but theological. The living interests of living souls are to be cared for; no reverence is due in the pulpit to the dreary combinations of abstractions known as theology. They are dead past resurrection, and should be allowed to rest in their graves. Most of the problems raised by theologians are unreal, and only need to be courageously neglected to be quite forgotten. You relegate some to the book of riddles, as Jowett said of problems in meta-

THE CLERICAL LIFE

physics, and some to the sphere of the mysterious, and go your way rejoicing.

Seriously, I think your joy is not so well grounded as I should like my friend's joy to be. Does it not occur to you that among all the needs which God has planted in us the most irrepressible and invincible is the need to think? Does it not make you yourself uneasy to have no conception of that truth as a whole which you minister to your people part by part? I should have a lower opinion of your intelligence than I have if I did not think so, and you may depend upon it that what you feel those who listen to you feel quite as much. No sane mind can be satisfied with *aperçus*. We like to catch a fresh glimpse of the truth here and there, to see it lit up with a ray from an unexpected quarter of the sky; but better than everything, because more satisfying to the deep sensitive mind of man, is it to feel that we see each several part as a part of the great whole of truth. An audience of ordinary people is far more keen in this respect than most speakers imagine. The common intelligence has a sense of unity, and misses it, and resents its absence, when it is not there. No partial truth tells as it ought to tell unless the hearer feels, as even a dull hearer can, that the pressure of the whole truth is behind it. You must not think to get out of this by saying that systematic construction of the whole truth is impossible to human intelligence. Very likely it is, but though you cannot be omniscient, one may surely plead that you should be coherent. And it is just the impression of incoherence, not so much in a single sermon as in your preaching as a whole, which is produced by your disregard of theology.

You have often said to me, and repeated it in preaching, that a dead dogmatic orthodoxy was responsible for much of current scepticism. Men brought up in an impossible theology cast off their theology and their Christianity together. That has its truths, but do you think, quite seriously, that a dead dogmatic orthodoxy will be so productive of sceptics as a type of Christianity which does not consider itself worth thinking about? Will earnest-minded men—and there are such in all our churches—take this new

Christianity to live and die by? If you think so, I do not. Now theology is the serious interpretation and construction in intellectual forms of all we know about God and man. We all need, crave for, and hail with gratitude, whatever helps us in this direction, and if you made the experiment of thinking your clearest, strongest, best and fullest, on any of the great 'dogmas' as you call them, 'truths' as I should call them, of the Christian revelation, I undertake to say you will find interest in quarters where you have failed to find it, and interest of a kind well worth attaching to the gospel. Our faith implies the grandest of all philosophies, and though one does not use philosophy to evangelise with, we ought to speak wisdom among the perfect, and help the minds of our people to feel at home in the great world of divine truth. There are, of course, incoherent mortals, eclectics, and others, who 'wear motley in their brains,' and who can only be caught with changing kaleidoscopic glimpses of truth, but luckily the mass of men are saner, and like their intellectual vesture not of patchwork, however gay, but woven of one piece from the top throughout. It is worth any pains so to master your own mind and experience so as to give the impression of such a unity and consistency in your preaching.

If you turn your mind to theology, too, it will vastly increase your interest in the Scriptures. You know very well, so well that you never conceal it, that you are not much at home in the epistles. You do get texts out of them occasionally, you condescend to select readings from them but you stumble at a great deal they contain. To speak frankly, that is because you only take texts from them. If the apostles were anything at all, they were theologians. They thought with an intensity which staggers us when we feel it, of what God had given them in Christ and in the Spirit, and of how this supreme gift stood related to the providential guidance of the world. Their mind can only be understood, can only be accepted or rejected, as a whole; and I for one am convinced that the chances of its acceptance rise immeasurably as we see how magnificent, how consistent, how profound and sublime a whole it is. Religion is a great thing, and even the plain man feels that the true preaching and interpretation of it must reflect its greatness. He has a sense for scale in ideas, and he misses in your non-theological preaching the grandeur of New Testament thought. In the effort to be interesting you too easily succeed in not being impressive. *Nova aliqua sed magna*, the younger Pliny begged his friend to write to him in his hour of sorrow; and the human soul everywhere goes out to that *sed magna*. Your practical, ethical, literary sermon, fresh as it may be, always leaves something—the essential something, the *magni aliquid* —to be desired; and I don't think you will be able to supply the want till you take the apostolic theology seriously, and find out the way to bring its greatness into your preaching. You are too sensible a man to be taken in by the nonsense that is talked about the independence of religion and theology; the Christian type of life and the Christian type of doctrine, at least in rational creatures, have some necessary relation to each other. The faith of the Christian, and his new life in faith, are far from perfection if they do not assert themselves in intelligence as well as in temper and conduct, and impel him to construct a Christian conception of God and man and the world in which his soul may find its rest. One may betray presumption in his procedure in this direction, no doubt; but to refuse to think consecutively, strenuously, and consistently, about what God has revealed to us in His Son and by His Spirit, is presumptuous in another way; the slothful man who declines the labour of thinking treats God as insolently as the man who thinks he has found Him out to perfection.

If you are not too angry, I will add one thing more. As a Christian minister it is your business to preach God to men. I have noticed in you and in other men who share your sympathies a certain want in this respect. You rather pride yourself on your knowledge of human nature, on your skill, won largely from the study of literature (and not to be won at all, as you tell me, from the study of catechisms), to read the heart and hold the mirror up to it: this is one of your great powers as a preacher. I grant it, but I should rather call it by another name. When you call it a great power, you mistake diagnosis

—not always of the deepest—for therapeutics. What a preacher needs, more even than the knowledge of man, is the knowledge of God. Without this, his ability to read the heart is the gift of the dramatist or novel-writer, not of the evangelist. Jesus knew what was in man, but that was not His gospel. He knew the Father. It is a serious thing to say, and I would not say it without feeling my responsibility, that your preaching has more of man than of God in it, and that it is evangelically ineffective for that reason. Think about God, what He is, what He has done, what He has promised to man; think out what is involved in the Incarnation, in the Atonement, in Christ's return as Judge; think of it all as a revelation of God, not merely as a ministry to man, and say, We praise Thee, O Lord, *propter magnam tuam gloriam.* These ancient words remind one of another thing also which you interesting non-theological preachers are apt to overlook to your own and the common loss; viz., that the Christian Church has a mind, a language and a style of its own, our part in which is lost unless we know theology to some extent both as a history and a science. Dr. Arnold of Rugby had a notion that a minister need no professional education; his vocation was simply that of a Christian gentleman whom the ordinary curriculum of the university fitted for his duties. It is not really so. The vocation is a unique one, and the intelligent fulfilment of it requires the minister to be a specialist in something. In what? In the knowledge of God, I should say; and that, in the mind, is theology. If it is in the mind, too, it will tell in the sermons; and I do not ask that it should do more.—Believe me, yours ever,

Nu.

VI

To a Minister whose Preaching is a Failure

To a Minister whose Preaching is a Failure

My dear Friend,—You complain with some bitterness that you are conscious of being a failure in the pulpit. I am not in the least surprised. To confess the truth to you, it would grieve or disgust me to be told the contrary. It would grieve me, if you are not grieved; it would disgust me, if you regarded your want of success with self-satisfaction. I readily and eagerly admit your failure may not be your fault. However much we may bewail it, it cannot be denied that this age is not favourable to the making of great preachers. It produces critics; and criticism, honest though it may be, means doubt. But preaching implies faith. The great critic is seldom, if ever, a great preacher; at least, not before he wins his way into the light. Then, indeed, he may be a greater believer and a greater preacher because of his doubt. And I am sanguine that the most powerful and brilliant period of the pulpit is before us. However that may be, the Church is now doing the pioneering work of the critics, and it must have the faith of patient waiting. Many a preacher, who is not an enemy of the higher criticism, finds its influence to be enervating. He feels, for instance, how hard it is to preach from the first chapters of Genesis. Were it not that we have the deep well of spiritual experience in the Psalms, it would often be too difficult a task to preach from the Old Testament. As to the New Testament, I believe the remark of a recent writer in *The British Weekly* is true, that we are turning the corner and entering on a time of greater certainty, stronger faith in dogmatic Christianity, and therefore more pulpit power.

It is true that you might avoid the necessity of passing through the present period of criticism, by the very ancient and very modern fashion of allegorical preaching. Allegory really is the prerogative of faith. When faith employs this method of teaching, it does so because it is sure of its steps. Bunyan allegorised in the exuberance of his faith. And Plato, I need not remind you, is never more ethically profound and spiritual than in his occasional myths. But the opposite is also true, that allegory is the refuge of the doubter. Some may think that the story of Er the son of Armenius, at the close of the Republic, is only a cloak over Plato's scepticism. That is not my opinion. Still, when a preacher turns the cities of the Plain, for example, or the journey of the Israelites through the wilderness, into a text for edifying lessons, he may do it for a very different reason from Bunyan. He may be hiding from the congregation, and, perhaps, from himself, his real unbelief, with words that have been the vehicle of faith. He preaches allegorically because he does not believe the actual history. What he does because of his own unbelief, our Lord did, when He spoke in parables, because of His hearers' unbelief, to whom it was not given to know the mysteries of the kingdom of heaven. But to you, as to the disciples, these mysteries are supposed to be in some measure revealed. If they are made known to you, speak them out 'plainly,' as what has been revealed unto you concerning the Father. Use parables with great caution. It is safer not to preach in allegory at all, unless, indeed, you are quite sure that you have a strong imagination and a strong faith. For it is certain you are not called to chastise your people's want of faith. Allegorical preaching is not for the use of the ordinary run of preachers, though they are the persons who find it the easiest, because the most idle, of all methods.

But, you say, I must not preach my doubts. No, but doubts hover midway between denial and belief. Some doubts end in denial. Others, however, have a face that is turned towards knowledge. The believing doubter—if I may be allowed the seeming paradox—is yearning for a truth which he has not found. When that is so, there is an evident progress from doubt to faith ; and, when such a man preaches, there is a conviction within him and within the hearts of his hearers that helps him and them to strive towards the better and nobler life. Though he may not believe *many* doctrines, those which he does

THE CLERICAL LIFE

believe he lays hold of with a firmer grasp. Do you not think that his will be powerful preaching? What I mean is that there is a reality underlying some doubting souls, while the doubts of another man are only the depth of a morass. Mr. Lewis Morris has said that Socrates 'doubted doubt away.'

Your failure, again, may lie at the door of your hearers. You are comparatively young, and have not been long in the ministry. It may be that you have not had time to educate your people to understand your teaching or to awake in them a consciousness of spiritual wants, which your teaching is calculated to satisfy. If that is the case, I pray you to remain strictly faithful to your present method of preaching. You are unpopular because of your hearers' false expectations. Wait. <u>Have the courage to be a failure</u>. Abate not one jot of what you demand from your hearers. Do not sacrifice the future to the present. You have to 'make' your people as well as your theology, but your theology first, and afterwards your people. And your people through your theology. The fatal mistake, which some **have** had to rue, is that they run before they have had a message, or when their message is insufficient or insufficiently understood by themselves. You were discreet enough to refuse a call from a church until your college course came to its natural termination, and have avoided the one-sidedness of others who are 'like a cake unturned.' You have a complete theology, whatever else you have not. You can look round an idea, and estimate its relation to other ideas. Now this, I take it, is of great importance for a preacher. It helps him with various kinds of hearers, at different stages of spiritual experience, or at no stage at all. It secures his own progress, without which he will be for a long time groping in the dark, like a belated traveller that has lost his way and cannot make out his bearings. Young preachers often fence with imaginary enemies. They are half-conscious that they are imaginary; else they would engage in a hand-to-hand conflict. They have no sense of proportion, no clear view of the end and aim of all their efforts. They are not 'synoptical,' as the old thinker has it. But *you* are in no danger

THE CLERICAL LIFE 73

of missing your mark. You will bring your people gradually to appreciate and adopt your own point of view; and, when you have conquered this initial difficulty, the rest will depend on yourself. One Sunday you will discover, to your own surprise and joy, that you and they understand one another. Then comes your opportunity.

But, whether the failure of which you complain is your own fault or your hearers', you know now why I am rather pleased than otherwise. A preacher that is satisfied with himself does not understand—to put it mildly—the work which he has to do. An advocate who has won his case, or a mathematician who has solved a problem, or an organiser who has bent the wills of other men to his own, may be naturally self-satisfied. But preaching belongs to another sphere. It is a fine art, as much as painting is, as distinguished from the mechanical arts, which become easier every day in the execution. You remember the remark of a certain painter, that he must have passed the zenith of his power, because he was now satisfied with his picture.

The observation of the author who complained that he had lost the genius that he had when he wrote one of his books is not so convincing to my mind. It may be that his consciousness of weakness arose from increased power. So the preacher is on the downward slope as soon as he is content with what he has achieved. In this respect preaching is like goodness. The greatest saints think that they are the greatest sinners, and the most effective preachers consider themselves the most conspicuous failures. Self-conscious satisfaction is never the mark of a great preacher. It would seem as if the act of self-contemplation were itself always and everywhere fatal to the consummate artist.

If this is true of preaching regarded as an art, how much truer must it be when we remember the nature of the particular work in which the preacher is engaged. His special business is to divest himself and his hearers of self, and fill himself and them with another Person's inspiration. As a mere orator, he draws inspiration from ideas. But preaching has a deeper source than even truths. It is part of the man's own godliness, and, like every other side of a pious character, must grow, yea, consciously fashion itself, after the pattern of the Incarnation itself. I was tempted to draw my pen through the words, '*consciously fashion itself*,' till I remembered the phrase used by the Apostle in the great passage that describes our blessed Lord's Incarnation. He does not hesitate to speak of Christ Jesus as 'emptying Himself' of the form of God that He might be able to take upon Himself the form of a servant. I do not here go into the reasons which satisfy my mind that the Apostle does not intend to say that Christ added the form of a servant to the form of God, as Lightfoot explains it, but means that He took the form of a servant instead of the form of God, as Meyer understands the words. Now, if our Lord *emptied* Himself voluntarily, deliberately, of His own accord, that He might begin a gradual process of growth, power, and glory, which would otherwise be absolutely closed against Him; if by omnipotence He cannot take man's intellect and heart by storm, but can and does by the self-emptying which is effected through Incarnation, shall we not say that the preacher achieves his highest triumph in the same way? Can we conceive a self-satisfied preacher of the emptiness of God other than a failure? How can he set forth the power of Christ's Incarnation? A preacher who has not the Incarnation for the staple of his sermons, whether he is conscious of it as a doctrine or simply knows its influence in moulding his own character, lacks the essential of powerful preaching; and the preacher who has it as a doctrine, but does not present the type of character which it ought to produce, is feeble and contemptible in the eyes of others, when he might and ought to be strong and glorious. Therefore take the comfort which your failure suggests.—Yours very faithfully,

EPSILON.

VII

To a Minister who is unsuccessful with Children

To a Minister who is Unsuccessful
with Children

DEAR MR. MEANINGWELL,—I have hesitated for some weeks before replying to the letter in which you kindly invite my opinion on your Sunday afternoon addresses to the children, and ask me for suggestions from my own experience as to the best means of interesting the young. My hesitation was chiefly due to the feeling that a retired minister like myself, who has settled as an ordinary member of a congregation, should keep himself rather scrupulously in the background, and should not in the slightest degree interfere with the pastor in his work. Since you wrote me I have visited a number of churches in the town, in order to see how the children's services are conducted, and though I frankly admit that your own methods do not altogether commend themselves to me, I fear there is very little you can learn from your neighbours.

At the parish church on Sunday afternoon I found an immense congregation of children assembled under the guidance of a young Irish curate. In each pew there were six or seven little boys or girls, with a teacher at the end or in the middle. Even so it was necessary for two men to walk up and down the aisles during the sermon, nudging one child, poking another, and frowning savagely at all. I watched carefully to see if a single boy or girl was taking any interest in the service, but, except in the front rows, not one was even pretending to listen. The little heads moved restlessly about; the hum of whispering grew louder at the dullest passages, until the curate came to a full stop and sharply called the congregation to order. The cause of his failure was not far to seek. He believes that the only method of interesting children is to adopt a style of extreme familiarity. His address was a kind of nursery talk, unattached to any definite subject, and interrupted by a number of foolish questions. The phrase, 'Now, children, listen to me,' must have recurred not less than fifty times. 'You have often seen a horse prick up its ears at a noise! cannot you try to do the same?' 'The children on the left are not answering my questions. Wake up, children, and hear what I am going to tell you about the Thames at Richmond. Has mother ever taken you to see the Thames? Yes, I am sure she has. Well, you saw the big river flowing along, but I wonder if you ever thought that it is not the same river which flowed along last year or last week in the same place. It is just like that with you, dear children. The hand which you, little Willy, held out to the master to be caned last week is not the same hand that you held out five years ago.' This is a fair specimen of the whole sermon. It meant nothing and led nowhere; the only lesson which resulted at the end was that children should cry as seldom as possible. 'What would you say about a little boy who cried for nothing? Would you not say that he was very silly? What would you say, children?' Faint murmurs from the front rows of 'Very silly.' 'Oh, but I want to hear all of you. Speak out, please, little girls on the left.' Every child in the church then shouted 'Very silly' at the

F

top of its voice, and the curate proceeded to enforce the great lesson of the afternoon—'You should laugh when you ought to laugh, and cry when you ought to cry.' This he made the children repeat after him several times, and when the noise was at the loudest I slipped out of my pew. There was still time to visit Holy Trinity in the next street, where the Low Church rector shares your opinion that children should not be left to Sunday-school teachers or superintendents, however able, but should be gathered into the church every Sunday afternoon, and instructed by the clergyman himself. The rector of Trinity, Dr. Ponderby, kept better order than the Irish curate, but he also was assisted by several stern men who patrolled the aisles. He preached a formal sermon from the pulpit, his subject being, 'Scenes from the Life of Elijah.' Each paragraph was introduced with the words, 'My youthful hearers.' One could not but feel that after such a sermon the children would never turn again with any interest to the life of the prophet. Dr. Ponderby cast the shadow of his own dulness over the Scripture page. He asked no questions, never called his audience to attention, never lifted his head from his sermon-case, and, except for his unvarying formula of address, seemed totally unconscious of any difference in age between himself and his audience. I have heard that Dr. Ponderby's grandfather, who was a chaplain to William IV., was famous for his sermons to the young. They were delivered twice a year, and attended by half of fashionable London. His form of address was, 'My young brethren.' It is said that Dr. Ponderby models his own discourses on his grandfather's. 'The all-important principle,' he has been heard to remark, 'is that the children of the poor should grow up to reverence the clergy.'

Mr. Selburne, of the Baptist Church, is rightly believed to have done more than any other man towards giving the children of our town a thorough knowledge of the Bible. His Schools have taken prize after prize in Scripture examinations. He tells me that his plan is to pack his children's sermons full of information, so that if the hearers miss the spiritual lessons, they shall at any rate carry something away. At my request he allowed me to look over one of his addresses.

The text was, 'I will lift up mine eyes unto the hills.' This served to introduce a description of the mountains of the Bible with approximate heights. The children were invited to find out and send to him in writing a list of events which are recorded to have happened on mountains.

'We have done the rivers and lakes of the Bible, the chief towns of Palestine, the scenery, and characteristics of Egypt, and the travels of the Apostles, during this winter,' said Mr. Selburne, with pardonable pride. 'Unfortunately our schools are somewhat falling off in numbers, possibly because we give so many home-lessons for preparation, but more probably because Mr. Andrews, of the Wesleyan Chapel, offers so many attractions in the way of treats.'

One afternoon I attended Mr. Selburne's class-room and examined the scholars, but although teachers and pupils seemed unusually earnest, intelligent, and well-informed, it was disappointing to find so many vacant seats. From my observations there, I am inclined to think that a pastor's relations to his young people should not be too severely intellectual.

THE CLERICAL LIFE 85

Mr. Andrews, the Wesleyan minister, is fortunate in having many rich and generous members. In summer and winter alike, constant amusements are provided for the children who attend his schools. A fortnight ago I looked in and heard the announcements at the close of the lessons. Mr. Andrews himself was present, and he stepped on to the platform with a friendly smile, which was answered by eagerly expectant looks from the children.

'I have a very pleasant announcement to make this afternoon, my dear young friends. Mr. Wontner, who has so often shown himself a kind friend to the school, wishes you all to have a happy day in the country. He has therefore invited the children with their teachers to tea in his beautiful park. We shall meet here at ten o'clock, and drive off in brakes which Mr. Wontner has kindly provided. Tell your fathers and mothers that Mr. Wontner would gladly have invited them to join you, but he fears there will not be room. Next year he hopes to organise a picnic for the parents. I trust you will all be punctual and regular in your attendance, so as to show that you appreciate the efforts of those who are trying to promote your health and pleasure, as well as your spiritual profit.'

Coming now to our own Church, I venture to think that you make the same mistake as Mr. Andrews, although in a different way. We are not a rich congregation, and we do not rely on frequent entertainments for filling our class-rooms. You appear to think, however, that the only method of attracting children is to give them amusing sermons, full of racy 'personal experiences.' You have an endless succession of anecdotes, most of which are taken from your own boyhood. 'Mother,' said a little girl of my acquaintance the other day, 'do you not think the minister must have been a very naughty boy?' We have heard how you robbed an orchard, how you ran away to sea, and how you played truant several times a week. 'As a boy, children, I was very fond of birds'-nesting, and I will describe to you a terrible adventure I once had in pursuit of this wicked amusement—an adventure which nearly cost me my life.' On my first Sunday in your church, I listened with breathless interest to your account of this 'adventure,' and I noticed that my grandchildren, who had never heard you before, were also much excited. They discussed the story at tea-time, and my youngest grandson declared, much to the astonishment of his nurse, that he meant to go to church twice every Sunday, 'to hear about the birds' eggs.' Next time you addressed the children you told how, as a boy, you longed to be an Indian. 'I am afraid, dear boys and girls, I was a wild and disobedient lad, and caused sad trouble to my poor father and mother.' We learned how, at the age of nine, you resolved to live in a wigwam, let your hair grow long and lanky, and steal out at night with a tomahawk to kill white strangers who had robbed the Indians of their land. My grandchildren were again deeply impressed. 'I think our minister's a *splendid* man,' said one of them that evening. But I noticed that the children who had been longer in the church were not particularly attentive. They had heard of too many adventures. Far be it from me to cast doubt on your veracity, but there is a strong suspicion that you did not really go through quite all these perils. When you stand in the pulpit and cheerfully announce, 'I well remember, children, how it was once the dearest wish of my heart to be a pirate and scour the seas under the black flag,' the children are conscious of a certain feeling of contempt. Your early life, if we may judge from your preaching, would furnish matter for a dozen penny dreadfuls.

A minister who desires the respect of children must show that he respects them. If there is listlessness and inattention in our church, it is because they have begun to doubt you. They regard you as a romancer, an Arabian Nights entertainer, the caliph of a hundred tales. Hardly a child believes seriously that at the age of fourteen you left home to enlist as a soldier, and that you met a good old man on the way, who persuaded you to abandon your purpose. That tale, if it stood alone, would have interested every one, but as you also left home at different times to be a sailor, a miner, and an engine-driver, its authority is not a little discounted. Personal experiences are excellent, but a man may have too many experiences. You will pardon me, I trust, for suggesting that we have heard different and contradictory accounts of the way in which you were first influenced for good. The old man on the Portsmouth road, who persuaded you not to join the army, was only one of many similar benefactors, who started up unexpectedly and in the nick of time. There was the old lady at a cottage window, with her Bible lying open before her, who called you back from a career of crime, and the preacher in the wayside chapel, who startled you with the words, 'What doest thou here, Elijah?' and the singer in the London streets, whose sweet voice melted your heart. Which of all these can we rely on? If you wish to recover your influence with the children, I should advise you to drop personal narrative. It may be true, as you say, that a preacher wins the heart of the young by himself living over again his youthful experiences. But in your case this principle has been carried too far. After you had harrowed our feelings with accounts of how you grieved and almost broke the hearts of your parents, we were not a little amazed by the very different accounts given by your father and mother when they visited the church last autumn. Your mother told every one that you had been a model son. Your father, addressing the Sunday-school, said it was always your dearest wish to be a minister. He remembered the book you loved best as a boy; it was the *Pilgrim's Progress*, which at eight you had learnt almost by heart. You were the best boy at day-school and Sunday-school, the pride of your teachers and an example to your class-mates. He might truthfully say that you had never cost your parents an hour's anxiety.

The facts, I suspect, lie somewhere between your father's description and your own. But these early reminiscences have served their purpose, and should now be thrown aside. The mere teller of stories is not the true preacher to children. Some fruits of the labour which you expend so freely for the benefit of the older people would be welcomed by your younger hearers. You are in no danger of becoming merely silly, like the Irish curate, or dull, like Dr. Ponderby, or cut and dried, like Mr. Selburne, or a caterer of meats and drinks, like Mr. Andrews. Give the children the best fruits of your mind and heart, and the results will repay you a thousandfold.—Yours,   X.

VIII

To a Ministerial Sir Willoughby Patterne

To a Ministerial Sir Willoughby Patterne

MY DEAR P.,—You had a cold last Thursday, and when you called at our house before the prayer-meeting, you remarked on the brevity of the most promising careers. 'I often picture to myself,' you said, 'my congregation as it would be on the Sunday after my removal. I seem to see the people all in mourning, the stranger in the pulpit, wearing my gown and handling my hymn-book and Bible. Not that I feel very ill, you added, 'but it is as well these things should be faced. There are few more terrible trials than the severance between a minister and an attached congregation.'

'Fortunately there is no question of that,' I murmured, for I knew of old your fondness for watching your own funeral.

'I think there ought to be a long interregnum

between two ministries,' you went on. 'It often amazes me to see how in three months a congregation can console itself. A church ought to pass through a lengthened widowhood. Nowadays the weeds are cast off before the grass is green on the pastor's grave.'

At the prayer-meeting we heard about McCheyne and Henry Martyn, and other eminent ministers who had been cut off in the flower of their days. Towards the end you asked, as you often do on such occasions, for leave to make a personal explanation. 'Owing to a severe cold which I caught in the rain last week I fear it will be impossible for me to preach on Sunday. The cold shows signs of settling on the chest, and my doctor advises me to take a few days' rest. I have therefore arranged that Mr. Lawson, of Barless, shall act as my substitute. It will, I know, be a severe trial to many of you to be deprived of my own ministrations, and I assure you that only grave physical causes would have led me away at such a time.'

Most congregations would have taken fright at your reference to 'grave physical causes,' but we have heard this 'Wolf, wolf' too often. Some months ago I, as your senior deacon, took alarm at your frequent references to some mysterious malady which might ere long leave us without a shepherd. I consulted your doctor, and to my unbounded satisfaction, learned from him that you have a thoroughly sound constitution, and are only inclined to be nervous. I wish, however, that you would not worry your wife with these imaginary ailments. The other day, I am told, you were heard saying that you would trust her to carry on your work among the people, and to see that your memory never faded from their hearts.

You have been our pastor nearly ten years, and you may rightly claim that under your ministry—'this ministry' is your favourite phrase—the church has prospered. The deacons have, however, an uncomfortable consciousness that you think them wanting in gratitude. Why need you tell us so often that the people of Ipswich, or Poole, or Warwick are envying our good fortune? Our late pastor did his duty in a quiet, steady way, letting us see that the advantages of our connection were mutual. You are always hinting that if in any particular matter you do not get your own way, 'other churches' will gladly offer you a more congenial sphere.

So far as I know, you have only had one call since you settled here in 1887. None of us could be ignorant on the subject, for the newspaper paragraph was posted by yourself to all the members. Shall I ever forget the church meeting which was called to deliberate on the matter? How you rang the changes on your sensitive nature, your need of sympathy, your feeling that many of us had not appreciated you. 'It would break my heart to leave,' you told us with plaintive emphasis. 'I am engaged in the training of many dear young people, who have learned to look up to me as their model. What would become of them if they were suddenly deprived of their counsellor and friend? Perhaps—I have been told so by not a few of the most cultured and intellectual among you—my preaching has a freshness not altogether common in these days of plagiarism and shallowness. Such powers as I possess are at your service; my only complaint is of your stony and indifferent silence. If my preaching

THE CLERICAL LIFE

profits you, write frankly and tell me so. I need encouragement more than most men. Mine is a self-distrustful, self-suspicious, self-condemning nature. If you wish to keep me among you, dear friends, do not leave me without the expression of your confidence. I make no claim to perfection, but while my poor gifts are spared me I shall gladly spend and be spent for your sakes.'

I think that speech first gave us a glimpse into the depths of your egoism. It is written of the immortal Sir Willoughby that his generosity roared of *I* louder than the rest, and such has been our experience. Have you ever attended a deacons' meeting without referring to the sacrifice you made in refusing an increase of stipend and the advantages of a larger town? The stipend exceeded ours by fifty pounds; the town has twenty thousand inhabitants for our ten. Surely, if we searched the history of Nonconformist pastorates, we might find a generosity even fit to match with yours.

You will not take it amiss, I trust, if I suggest that we have now heard enough about the books and the men that have influenced you. It was interesting at first to know that you traced the vigour of your prose style to a careful study of Carlyle's *French Revolution*, that your peculiar aptitude for dividing texts had been acquired from Dr. Maclaren, and that as a boy you had learned by heart two books of *Paradise Lost*. But your habit of giving obituary notices of great men in your Sunday evening sermons, with particular reference to the influence they exerted on your own development, has now become wearisome. When Mr. Spurgeon died, your only allusion was a reminiscence of how he had once (by accident, I suppose) heard you address a meeting, and had said afterwards, 'That young man has the making of a preacher.' We have heard that tale at least two hundred times.

Do you remember your excitement when a newspaper offered to interview you? Before that time you had spoken of interviewing and of journalism in general with profound contempt. 'Mark my words,' you said one evening, 'if ever the papers propose to interview me, I shall absolutely decline. Could anything be more undignified than for the leaders of denominations to give themselves away in such a fashion? When my opinions are presented to the world, it shall be through the medium of some eminent publishing house.'

Time passed on, and last winter you organised a very useful soup-kitchen. It was a new departure in our county, and the *Daily Mirror* wrote asking leave to interview you on the subject. At ten o'clock I met you on your way to the post-office.

'The *Daily Mirror* requests an interview,' was your breathless greeting.

'Indeed! but of course you will refuse?'

'Not at all. I dislike interviewing in the abstract, but in this case the circumstances are peculiar. The congregation has a right to expect that its work shall be made known.'

Before the day closed, every member knew that you had called at the office and answered the questions of the interviewer. With burning eagerness we looked out next day for the article. To our amazement there were only three sentences about the soup-kitchen; the rest was your own personal and family history. Facts which we knew were there—the story about Mr. Spurgeon, the study of Carlyle, the learning of *Paradise Lost*. But we were not aware that your father—who kept a small shop at West Wilmington—was a man of marvellously retentive memory and of exquisite literary taste, and that you inherit your pulpit gifts from him. Neither had we noticed that our chapel is so crowded on Sunday evenings that the doorkeeper has often to turn hundreds away. To the best of my knowledge this has happened only once in the history of the church—on the night when Dr. V—— introduced you. You edified your interviewer, if I remember rightly, with the remark that all really great sermons are founded on personal experiences. 'No study of Biblical characters delights my people so much as the simple records of my own private history.' Like Sir Willoughby, you might have added, 'Our nature is mysterious, and mine as much as any.'

May I venture, with great deference, to suggest that your 'personal experiences' have been surprisingly numerous. You are now thirty-eight; you came to us in 1887; yet if ever there was a man with a past, you are he. Did you really take that journey in Northern Russia and Spitzbergen in the depth of an Arctic winter? Is it possible that at the age of eighteen you addressed a vast audience in one of the largest chapels in the Midlands? Did you actually, when your income was only £70, spend two-thirds of it on books and magazines? A kind of legendary glow has gathered round your earlier years; but when you spoke last Sunday morning of dining twelve years ago at the table of your friend Baron —— in Norway, your natural acuteness must have detected the look of doubt on our faces. Some day, if time is granted, we expect to hear of your journeyings in Mexico, South Africa, and Spain.

Our older members are becoming alarmed by your vague references to the Higher Criticism: 'On the whole, I am disposed to agree with Wel'hausen'; 'My judgment is at one with Canon Cheyne's as to the date of the Psalter.' As you never tell us what the conclusions of these eminent scholars are, our minds are left in a state of blank bewilderment.

Before closing, I may mention one other point. You asked me to read at the Literary Society to-morrow the paper you had promised to deliver, entitled 'A Post-card from Mr. Gladstone.' On examining the paper, I think it might be best to make the excuse of your cold, and allow the young men for once to get up an impromptu discussion. The Society does not care to know the whole history of your mental education on the Home Rule question. If you considered it worth while to write and ask Mr. Gladstone whether he believed the Act of Union was passed by corrupt methods, you need not, I think, have made the fact of his replying 'Yes' on a post-card an excuse for wasting two hours of the Society's time. Neither will the circumstance that you were a Home Ruler before Mr. Gladstone be of much practical service to the Irish cause.

We appreciate your excellent qualities; we wish to retain you as our pastor for many years. But—you will pardon an old man for saying so—an Egoist wears out the patience of his truest friends.—Yours, etc., **X.**

IX

To a Minister who regards himself as a Prophet of Criticism

To a Minister who regards Himself as a Prophet of Criticism

Dear Newlyte,—It was very friendly to take me into your confidence to-day, and I gave my mind to the situation last night when the traffic had ceased on the street and the firelight was weaving mystical patterns on the floor. One is wiser then than at any other hour, because one is quieter and can hear the Inner Voice.

Accept, first of all, the assurance of my unaffected sympathy in this cross providence that has befallen you. It was a brave idea to share with your people unto the uttermost the fruits of your critical study; it must have been a bitter disappointment to find that they repaid you with distrust and suspicion. Your bookcase ledges and three tables hardly able to sustain the open volumes of criticism—Wellhausen looking very stodgy—and your anxious figure flitting from book to book, trying to reconcile blazing contradictions, make an interior that has as yet escaped art, but will some day afford a companion picture to the Alchemist. The scene came up vividly before my eyes, and affected me by its irony of circumstances. Your neighbour Foodle, who believes that Solomon jotted down Proverbs as a kind of private diary in the intervals of pleasure, and who recently explained to a deeply impressed conference that after Isaiah's lips were burned away the Lord spoke through him as if he were a funnel, preached last Sunday on the Atonement from the text of the 'badgers' skins,' and has been going from house to house for a week sipping honey, while you wandered for four days and part of two nights through a sandy desert of documents in order to prove that Moses could not have written Deuteronomy, and have received on an average six letters a day ever since from aggrieved members of your congregation, lamenting your fall, besides one from 'A Well-wisher,' pointing out kindly but firmly that an avowed atheist is hardly a fit person to be the minister of a

Christian congregation. It does seem as if justice were indeed blind which crowns pious laziness with favour and thrusts honest work into the pillory, and I quite understand that you are tempted to regard religious opinion with contempt, especially if it be orthodox.

You will, however, pardon me for suggesting that your indignation ought not to have been poured on that benevolent-looking man who preceded me in your study, and to whom you appear to have expressed your mind with much freedom. Granted that he never had the benefit of University culture, and has not even our antiquated authority Ewald in his house; granted that he has the misfortune to be rich and to hold conservative views in faith. Let us indeed admit at once, as you seemed to have hinted to him more or less politely, that he was a Philistine and bourgeois to the backbone. Still he has something to say in this matter, and was not of necessity guilty of impertinence in his remonstrance. Unless I am mistaken, he gave largely to build your handsome church, and has backed you up in all your work with hearty goodwill.

He is well known in the city as an honourable, able, modest man—one who has brought great credit on the Christian name. No one has ever called him a fool or a hypocrite. Remember also that a man of affairs is more likely than a scholar to form a sane judgment on the drift of things. If that kind of man is alarmed, you may take for granted that he has reasonable cause, and it was not good manners, to say the least, to pelt him with critical jargon and refuse him reasonable satisfaction. Perhaps you are the only man living that would treat him with insolence, and you are his minister and might be his son. Excuse this plainness; it is not his white hair, although one need not be ashamed to show respect to age, it is rather his face, as I saw it on the stair, which stirs me. It was of one who had suddenly lost a friend.

Do not fling down my letter at this point and become heroic, protesting that no one has a right to dictate what you are to preach, and that you will not sell your conscience for gold. Make a manly effort and refuse the luxury of a parallel between yourself and Galileo. It is a little hackneyed and entirely out of correspondence. You will not be persecuted or put out of your church if you persist in re-editing the Old Testament. That worthy man will quietly slip away to some place where the drone of the Hexateuch is not heard, leaving his heart behind him, and a number of old-fashioned people will disappear. Your congregation may become small, but this will not be because people are afraid of the light; it will be because your sermons are so tiresome; a few will always remain for the sake of your wife and children. Disabuse your mind of the idea that you are a martyr; your congregation will be the martyrs.

My heart grew very tender in the end to the old saints in your church, who do not write nasty letters or talk against you, who love and pray for you. They have inherited certain ideas about the form of the Bible which may be inaccurate —and there you and I might agree—but which they cannot now exchange, and you set yourself to explode them every second Sunday for the space of a year. Worship in St. Origen's is like living in the Riviera during the earthquake season; you never know what wall in your villa will crack next, and it gets on the nerves. The twenty-third Psalm used to be a green pasture, but now you have turned it into an opportunity for drawing a parallel between David and Robin Hood, with the view of showing the improbability of the Book of Psalms coming from a bandit. The very name of Isaiah makes the pews to tremble, for you began with two prophets, and now no one can calculate the number of anonymous writers that have gone to complete the book. And I think you yourself felt afterwards that it was a mistake to take the 53rd of Isaiah for a sermon on Good Friday, and discuss the identity of the servant of the Lord for forty minutes, with only a casual reference to Christ. One may not be an obscurantist, and yet be a little weary of this pedantry.

You explained to me that you had a mission, and that you dared not hold your peace. 'How shall I answer to God at the last if I keep back truth or leave my people in ignorance?' When a man rises to that height, one can only say, 'Quite so,' but a plain person may be pardoned if he tastes the humour of the situation. We are overrun with prophets nowadays and grotesque missions; but perhaps the most amazing prophet that ever claimed to have a mission from God is the preacher who arises to dispel the myth of the Davidic Psalms, or explain the difference between the Jehovist and Elohist documents. Where would this poor world be if that voice were silent? 'Behold, the darkness shall cover the earth, and gross darkness the people!' May it not be that you are taking yourself too seriously, and that you might abandon this high walk without treachery to conscience? You have read a fair number of books, and you have a just estimate of your abilities, but one may conclude, without offence, that you are not a critic at first hand or an expert scholar. If you were, it would be necessary for you to resign your charge without delay, both for the sake of scholarship and your congregation. As you are not, it is worth your serious consideration whether you are justified in hindering your general practice by semi-amateur specialism. Unload any useful Bible criticism in your classes, and let the pulpit go free. Why should you forfeit the power of your preaching to be a sixth-rate Biblical critic?

My belief is that you are largely influenced in this unfortunate effort by the fact that a handful of sceptical people sit in your church. They are not five per cent. of the congregation, but their presence makes you self-conscious and serves to deflect your thought. Something especially liberal and intellectual must be placed before this company, and you have gone hunting in the wastes of criticism for their food. Are you perfectly certain that this class will be carried captive by a Bible you treat ostentatiously as ancient literature, or that after hard brain work during the week they hunger for new problems on Sunday? Could they not read Kuenen for themselves, if this be their soul's desire, and is it not possible that they have come to you for guidance and stimulus in the spiritual life? May it not have been the soul of the Bible that has attracted these aliens, and you have dissected its body for their edification? They came for bread, although they did not say so, and, with the best intentions in the world, you have offered them a stone.

So far I had written on Saturday; but as no one ought to send a letter to a hard-worked minister on that day, I laid down my pen before the signature, and now I congratulate myself on the delay. Let me thank you with all my heart for this morning's sermon, which has given me and many others a great lift in the good way of God. When you announced your text from the Book of Isaiah, a weary look came into many faces, for the Evangelical prophet had been robbed of his charm; but as you read the words, 'Ho, every one that thirsteth,' we lifted our heads at the ring in your voice—the old note of the Evangel—and a wistful, expectant look came into our friend's face. Before you had spoken five minutes the hearts of the people were as one, and ere you had finished strong men were moved to their depths. Coming out, I overheard that good man say to a neighbour, 'I'm going from home for two months, and I shall leave with a glad heart,' and your F.R.S. declared to me that it was the best sermon he had heard for many a day. 'What one desires from a preacher in this day,' he added, 'is not information, but faith.'

You have come into the trade winds at last; up with every sail, and God prosper you.—Yours faithfully, LAMBDA.

X

From a Minister who is asked to many Tea-parties

From a Minister who is asked to many Tea-parties

DEAR MR. SOTHERBY,—As we had a chat this evening at Mrs. Lapham's, you will be surprised to get a letter from me by to-morrow morning's post. I am writing to you, not as a deacon of the church, but as an old and tried friend, who has shown me many kindnesses from my student days until now. I wish to ask your advice on a matter of some importance.

There is an impression in our congregation that a minister is a man of unbounded leisure. Because I do not travel with you to the City every morning, and return by the six o'clock train in the evening, people suppose that my time is unoccupied. The result is that I receive daily invitations to 'At Homes,' tea-parties, and family gatherings. No one is more assiduous in her attentions than our friend Mrs. Lapham. My sister Charlotte tells me that Mrs. Lapham considers me unsociable, and thinks that my manners need improvement. This evening she drew my sister into a corner by herself, and remarked what a pity it was that Mr. Silcox did not go more into society. 'We are all fond of him, my dear; we like his preaching; and, of course, it is pleasant to have a University man and a scholar for one's minister, but it is too bad of your brother to shut himself up in his study and to refuse to see us in our homes. How can he do any real good unless he knows his people personally? Besides, you must excuse me for hinting that a young man of twenty-five needs to have his manners polished by intercourse with the world. Our late pastor, Dr. Allen, had most courtly manners. There was something majestic in his bow, and he lifted his hat like the Prince of Wales. He never thought it beneath him to drop in upon his members. During his later ministry he made a practice of coming to tea with our family at least twice a week. Of course, we should not demand so much attention from your brother,

THE CLERICAL LIFE

but once a fortnight he might surely spend half an hour at my " At Home.'"

I have a bundle of notes in my desk received at different times from Mrs. Lapham. One asks me to come to tea because her eldest girl is home from school; another because the family have returned safely from their summer holiday at Boulogne. I was invited again when Aunt Martha came to visit them from Manchester, and also when Bob and Harry wished to let me see their bicycles. When no family excuse is forthcoming, Mrs. Lapham hopes I will call to talk over the little trouble in the choir, or to consult as to whether a series of special meetings should not be immediately organised. When I go to Mrs. Lapham's I usually find about half of our members assembled. My time is thus not altogether wasted, for I can do a certain amount of pastoral work in this way. The ladies who frighten me most are those who ask me to *tête-à-tête* tea-drinkings. One of these is Miss Belhurst, who sends a confidential note about once in three weeks by the hands of her little servant. The note is sealed with black sealing-wax, and has

'Private' marked in large letters on the envelope. Inside it runs somewhat like this:—

'DEAR MR. SILCOX,—I know your time is much occupied; but as there is a private matter on which I am anxious to talk with you, I shall be pleased if you can come to tea at five o'clock this afternoon.'

The first time I accepted Miss Belhurst's invitation, I found that she wished to criticise my Sunday evening's sermon. 'I am one of your oldest members, and you must not complain if I find your preaching scarcely equal to Dr. Allen's. There is, it seems to me, a certain want of definiteness. Not that I find any actual fault, I am conscious merely of a vague feeling of uneasiness. In these days of doubt and criticism—but here comes Lizzie with the muffins and the buttered buns, and I must keep the little present I had prepared for you till after tea.' The little present consisted of five bulky manuscript books, containing Miss Belhurst's notes of Dr. Allen's sermons. She recommended me to study them carefully, and mould my style on Dr. Allen's. On another occasion Miss Belhurst sent for me because she had been much impressed by my sermon on 'Secret Trials.' She wondered if I could have intended it for her, as at that moment she was suffering from a cruel trouble, of which she had not breathed a word to any one. The truth was, her poor brother William had decided to marry a lady ten years older than himself and with no money. Miss Belhurst asks my advice about investments, and during the recent American crisis sent for me at ten o'clock one evening to know whether she should sell out her New York railway shares. Once I gently hinted that my congregation were responsible for wasting much of my time. 'Yes, indeed,' she replied, 'I have often wondered at Mrs. Lapham's inconsiderateness.'

Other kind friends who have lately found excuses for asking me to tea are Mrs. Brock, who has set up a boarding-house, and wished to introduce me to her first visitors ; and Miss Macintyre, who has settled in a flat. We have, as you know, several ladies' boarding-schools connected with the church, and it seems a little hard that I should be expected to attend their breaking-up parties every term. I am hopelessly unmusical, yet the head teacher rushes up as I am leaving, and begs me to wait another half-hour to hear Agnes play 'The War March of the Priests' in *Athalie*, or to listen to little Aileen's wonderful performance on the violin.

I have tried my best to please these hospitable friends; but from what my sister tells me, the church is honeycombed with jealousies. This evening I find a note from Miss Belhurst, earnestly hoping she has done nothing to offend me, as I had refused to take tea with her on Wednesday, and yet her servant had seen me go into Mrs. Lapham's this evening. Miss Playfair, principal of one of the ladies' schools, trusts I will not desert her this Easter as I did last year; for she attributes the slight falling off in the numbers to the fact that I went to Miss Padge's and Miss May's schools, but was in Birmingham on the day of her 'entertainment.'

The letters I dread most are those which begin with apologies. Here is a specimen of them:—

'DEAR MR. SILCOX,—We all know a minister's time is valuable, and that the study, not the drawing-room, is your congenial sphere, but my husband—and you know what a busy man *he* is—thinks you take too little recreation. He therefore joins with me in hoping that you will not think it a great liberty if we ask you to come to us to-morrow at four. We have just had several chests of tea from Ceylon, where our son is a planter, and we are anxious that you should try it. If dear Miss Charlotte will accompany you, we shall feel you are both doing a great favour to our boy, who, by the way, was a constant admirer of your preaching.—Yours very sincerely, L. E.'

I was unfortunately prevented from tasting L. E.'s Ceylon tea; but Charlotte met this lady about a week ago, and was informed that it was very doubtful whether the family would be able to remain in connection with the congregation, as their business was increasing so rapidly that they were thinking of moving to the West End.

Can you do anything to protect me from these

invitations? My list for next week is longer than ever. On Monday I have promised to take tea with old Mrs. Ledwell, to celebrate the news of her son's safety in the Transvaal. On Tuesday, Miss Belhurst hopes I will look in for half an hour, as it is her fifty-seventh birthday, and she feels lonely with none of her relatives near her. Mrs. Lapham reminded me this evening that Wednesday was her quarterly tea-drinking for the girls of her Bible-class, who were looking forward to an evening with their minister. On Thursday, Mrs. Brock hopes I will spare time to take tea at her boarding-house, as she specially wishes to introduce to me a young gentleman of wonderful artistic talent, who, with a little timely assistance, would become a famous painter.

For some time I had a feeling of warm respect and admiration for the Achesons, the new family who settled in the church last autumn. I saw almost nothing of them, but instinctively I regarded them as friends. I turned with a positive relief from the pews of those with whom I had drunk tea on Friday, or expected to drink tea on Monday, to this sensible, considerate household from whom I had never once received an invitation. Alas! when I came home from Mrs. Lapham's this evening, the first letter I opened was from Mrs. Acheson. They were new people, she said, and had feared it might be taking a liberty to ask the pastor to tea. She trusts, however, I will come next Friday evening, when she and her husband will have pleasure in showing me several curious idols and strings of shells sent home by her brother, who is a missionary in the South Seas.

You will understand that I find myself in a somewhat serious dilemma ; and as my lady friends refuse to take pity on me, I must throw myself on the kindness of the deacons, and especially of yourself. My only hope of success in this church is to devote my time to my proper work of study and preaching, and I wish you would let it be known that I find it impossible to attend any further tea-drinkings.—Yours very truly,

HENRY SILCOX.

XI

To a Young Minister who refused to wear a White Tie

To a Young Minister who refused to wear a White Tie

MY DEAR P.,—The report of your induction services has interested me greatly. I am delighted that you can send such a cheering account of your settlement and its prospects, social and spiritual. One sentence in your letter moves me to reply sooner than I might otherwise have done. You say, *inter alia*, that after careful consideration you are quite resolved never to wear a white tie, which you describe as 'a wretched rag of clericalism.' I presume you will relax this rule at dinner-parties, and appear then like everybody else. Your vow only applies to those times and seasons when the ordinary man's necktie is not white. Well, you have some excellent precedents for your departure in Mr. Spurgeon and Dr. Dale, not to mention minor prophets. I am not sure whether they and you have perfectly reconciled theory and practice in this matter of ministerial costume. Few of us are entirely consistent with our dearest principles; and I suspect that even you will not stand up to preach in the light summer suit and parti-coloured cravat which are usual among the laity of your own age. It is curious how innocently that poor 'rag of clericalism' began. Early in this century the white neckcloth was common to all professional men; the lawyer and the physician as well as the parson. I remember myself an ancient doctor, and a still more ancient solicitor, who preserved the custom of their youth, and never wore anything else. But in our day it survives only among ministers of religion, and in this way it has become practically their outward and official badge. You reject it, because you dislike what Mr. Ruskin calls 'an offensively celestial uniform.' And I have heard you confess your instinctive dread lest you should degrade into a religious official.

And yet, after all, my dear P., be honest and say whether you have not, as a matter of fact, joined this clerical class, of which the white tie is a recognised conventional symbol. You have had some years of training at a theological college to fit you for this special task. You have been appointed to a distinctive office in your Church, whose functions are *sui generis* ; and by virtue of that office you take a corresponding public rank in your town. You are already drawing a regular stipend (I only wish it were larger) from your position as a Christian minister. You will forgive me for writing thus frankly. I know that you dislike the idea of being paid for doing good. There seems to you—as to many high-minded men—something like degradation in taking money for spiritual service. St. Paul allowed it, indeed; but he mostly refrained from using his own permission. And if you had your way, you would prefer to go tent-making with St. Paul, or spectacle-making with Spinoza.

It is perfectly true that a minister often pockets a good deal of pride, which is near akin to self-respect, when he accepts a salary. But the differentiation of functions in modern life is such that 'separated ministers' are as indispensable for the Church as officers are for the army. And neither of the two classes need be ashamed of drawing their pay. It would be sheer waste of time for you to go and earn your living at some drudgery, and then to give the margin and remnant of your energies and leisure to the service of the Church. If only on the grounds of simple economy of labour you consent to be 'set apart;' and, moreover, if you had no admitted fitness for the work —if you felt no peculiar vocation for it—you would not venture to become a minister at all.

Now I entirely sympathise with your own feeling that out of this necessary and inevitable separateness there arises a real danger. All the history of the Church proves how easily the pastor and the prophet gravitate into the priest. And to repudiate sacerdotal theories is no guarantee against the fatal spirit of professionalism *was uns alle bändigt*, and whose taint creeps over the heart unawares. Why, the very familiarity of a religious teacher with what is sacred is apt to harden and coarsen his own inward sensibility. The late Mr. George Dawson was the most anti-clerical of men; yet of him George Eliot wrote regretfully: 'I imagine it is his fortune, or rather misfortune, to have talked too much, and too early, about the greatest things.'

THE CLERICAL LIFE

'Is there no danger' (asks Maurice) 'that we shall play with the most dreadful words as if they were counters, shall use the names of Heaven and Hell and of God Himself as if they were mere instruments of our trade? Is there no danger that there shall be nothing answering in our acts to our words, that we shall be more grovelling than ordinary men in one, in proportion as we are more magnificent in the other?' I am glad that you do feel this danger; but surely it lies in the nature of the situation itself; it is absolutely independent of any accidents of costume.

You will find, indeed, that it is one peculiar hardship of a minister's calling that he dare not permit himself to share that immense relief which comes to other men from mere routine. A medical student, for instance, gets so habituated to the dissecting-room that his first natural revulsion is lost in the absorbing interest of his study. The most tender-hearted doctor learns to suppress his sympathies for the sake of his work. A surgeon cannot afford to have nerves; he grows efficient as he is able to operate mechanically, without regard for the pain that it is his duty to inflict. But take the case of a minister who has to listen to confessions of sin, such as come uninvited to every good shepherd of souls. No task is more repulsive, and it must never grow less repulsive. You dare not let familiarity with the details of moral disease dull and deaden your hatred of what is itself wrong. Whatever skill you may gain to deal with such a case will be in exact proportion to your delicate conscience and your keen, passionate sensibility to evil. If you once come to look at sin in a merely professional light, you will have lost your power as a spiritual guide. The routine which brings such merciful relief to other men's work is for you a continual snare.

There are other drawbacks in belonging to the clerical class. The sense of it creates a subtle, invisible barrier between ordinary people and the parson. They stand mentally aloof from you. They use reserve. They are hardly ever quite natural. They treat you, half unconsciously, like a creature of a different order from themselves. They behave as though there were no exceptions to the old epigram which has divided humanity

THE CLERICAL LIFE 135

into three sexes—men, women, and parsons. Even your friends in your own congregation, who repudiate the theory of a priesthood as vigorously as you do yourself, will quietly try to thrust orders upon you by a kind of informal plebiscite. They like their minister, as they say, to be a minister. And without meaning it they will do their best to turn his human influence, his natural spontaneous example, into a formal, artificial, professional thing.

You see that I do not underrate the characteristic difficulties of your recognised position as a Christian teacher. That position brings any man subtle perils and delicate intoxications peculiar to itself. The danger of professionalism is one of the easiest and deadliest. But that danger has only the most shadowy connection with the presence or absence of a white tie. *Cucullus non facit monachum.* The temptation to legal casuistry would remain unimpaired in the law courts even if Her Majesty's judges decreed that no barrister need henceforth wear a wig. You must not exaggerate a trifling detail of costume as though it determined the habit and temper of your inner self. If not now, at any rate when you grow older, you will recognise that in such outward forms it is generally wiser to take that course which the tradition of our country or our Church suggests, because that 'implies less of self-dependence and self-will.'

And there is a real danger in this revolt against whatever seems professional, lest you should think that you need not be different from ordinary people—that you ought not to be better than the crowd. Whatever garments you don or doff, the fact remains that you are a man consecrated and set apart, called to the most sacred office, trained for the highest work on earth. From one point of view you cannot be too genial, too brotherly, too humane. But from the other point of view you can very easily become too worldly, too secular, too much like common men in tone and speech and style and manner. The indispensable thing about Holy Orders is not the ordination but the holiness. The white flower of a blameless life is far more distinctive than any costume, and the pure heart, kept unspotted from the Church as well as the world, will stamp you unmistakably as a priest of the Most High God.

OMICRON.

XII

*To a Minister who becomes periodically
'Run Down'*

To a Minister who becomes periodically 'Run Down'

My dear B.,—I am happy to hear that you have carried home a fresh stock of vigour from our sunshine and sea-breezes. In this quiet village few people arrive to quicken one's memories and interests as you did during the fortnight which you made so enjoyable to your host. May I take an old man's privilege, and write what has been on my mind ever since you left me last week? From what I saw of you here, as well as from what you let fall about your habits in our long rambling conversations, I am seriously concerned lest you should drift into a chronic state of 'slackness'—physical and mental—simply through bad management of yourself. You are happy in having a sound constitution, a congenial profession, a healthy district, and no family troubles. Yet you confess that you are constantly getting 'out of sorts'; you often drag on for weeks 'with all the wheels of being slow'; your work is done wearily and haltingly; the spirit is languid and the flesh is indisposed; and without being actually ill, you miss all the spring and zest which make life worth living to a man of your age. Not that you have any disease; you talk about 'brain-fag,' but your doctor has assured you again and again that your only ailment is 'being below par.' And, as you keep up your wholesome prejudice against stimulants, he drenches you with tonics and prescribes more extra holidays than you can possibly afford to take. Will you forgive me for saying that you can almost certainly cure yourself if you choose, and that it is your very serious duty to try? No spiritual gifts can absolve a minister from the elementary obligation to keep his body and mind at their highest possible pitch of efficiency for the work which is given him to do. For though a man cannot be uniformly at his best, yet I am certain that the inferior preacher who is at his best has far more momentum than the pulpit genius who is 'out of sorts' and 'run down.' The secret of many a dull, slovenly, futile sermon

THE CLERICAL LIFE 141

is the depressed vitality of the minister. To fulfil your vocation you must steadily endeavour after what Browning defined as 'a life lived at the top of the wave'; whereas at present you are far too apt to lie tossing and weltering uneasily in its trough.

Of all men that I know you are readiest to scoff at Manichean superstitions; and yet even you fall short of a full Christian faith in the worth and dignity of the human body. You drop unawares into that quite common heresy which made St. Francis call his body 'Brother Ass,' and treat it accordingly as a drudge, to be ignored so long as it did not absolutely break down. But 'the soul's dark cottage' has become a shrine which we are forbidden not only to defile, but to misuse or to neglect. Is not one practical Christian duty to 'present our bodies,' and therefore to preserve our bodies, day by day, in the best possible condition? The fisher of men will find himself a very incomplete angler if he takes no pains to keep himself in what sportsmen call 'good form.' What you need— for your work's sake—is to go into regular training, and to make your food and drink, and exercise and recreation, and study and prayer, all combine to fit you for the cure of souls.

> 'Let us not always say,
> "Spite of this flesh to-day
> I strove, made head, gained ground upon the whole!"
> As the bird wings and sings,
> Let us cry, "All good things
> Are ours, nor soul helps flesh more, now, than flesh helps soul!"'

The truth is, you secretly despise the details of living. You pay no regard to the management of yourself. You fancy it a noble Spartan virtue to neglect your body; and so, without being an ascetic, you just go on carelessly, casually, while the mechanism is continually running down through sheer inattention. For instance, you were confessing to me how rarely you keep any sort of rule as to bedtime, so that sleep grows shy of such an erratic wooer, and you wake next day jaded and depressed. We should hear of fewer nervous breakdowns if men understood that regular sleep is as important as regular food. As to exercise, I have heard you plead the hoary old excuse—you are too busy. That may be quite true, but it is quite invalid. You have no business to be so busy. You will double your real efficiency when you cancel half your small engagements. It is shortsighted, as well as unapostolic, to turn yourself into a parochial 'handy man.' Believe me, the snare of the *fin-de-siècle* parson is to attempt everything himself; and as a penalty, he manages to do nothing better than some one else could do it in his stead. You are a Christian specialist, and on the very lowest ground you cheapen your office, as well as dissipate your energy, by this endless entanglement in petty local affairs; it is fatal to the mental aloofness and spiritual detachment which your proper work requires. That work can never be done as it deserves while you go on living under the harassing strain of burdens which are no part of your real duty. After all, you were not educated and ordained to be an Extension lecturer, or an election agent. Faith and expediency alike call you away from these side issues, that you may have leisure and vigour to spare for the greatest things of all.

You see I give you full credit for an industrious spirit, though I am afraid you have still to learn the economics of ministerial energy. It struck me irresistibly that your work was like that of a machine with loose bearings and couplings. I suspect that you want steadily and resolutely bracing up. A minister can generally arrange his day's work pretty much according to his own taste and fancy as regards the clock. But it is a real temptation to have no settled hours for settled duties. I remember a High Church vicar telling me how thankful he was for his daily service at church, because, he said, 'you know that you have at any rate got one duty in each day definitely fixed for you.' I expect that you are apt to fix nothing in particular, and consequently to feel disinclined for everything in general.

You are a bachelor, and so not exposed to those domestic distractions which sometimes invade a parson's study so much more wantonly than they would intrude into a barrister's chambers. But you are all the more liable to the aimless, amiable visitor who looks in to see if you are as idle as himself. You can never charge your mind with any subject unless you keep it properly insulated ; and you are bound to be intolerant of interruptions which lead the current to earth. 'Enter into thy closet, and shut-to the door'—it is the only way to concentrate yourself, and often it requires a severe effort of will.

One chief evil of physical depression is that the brain is less nimble and alert to obey ; you get into that slip-shod state of mind which feels fit for nothing better than a newspaper and a pipe. 'Mental inertia'—our grandfathers called it an uglier name—is a familiar fiend which haunts the study ; but even it can be exorcised by a will resolutely bent on doing the Father's business. Who dare dawdle over such a task? Is it too much to expect that the man thus occupied shall make himself 'business-like,' shall cultivate those elementary habits of diligence and punctuality and concentration which every merchant requires in his office, and which are not less necessary in the search for the goodly pearl and the hid treasure? Yet some ministers seem to regard casualness as a fine art ; they accept it as the outward token of genius or sanctity ; they are

K

incapable of such vulgar duties as keeping appointments and answering letters. Yet to be casual is always to be selfish. By these unbusiness-like habits a man not only makes himself incompetent and unreliable, he simply throws upon others the extra burden of taking the pains which he refuses to take. I know quite well that you have a conscience on this subject; but I am afraid it is generally a reproachful conscience. You have got into such a slack way of doing things that your correspondence is aways in arrears, and your engagements continually arrive before you are ready. You feel all the time that instead of being master of your work, you are letting your work miserably tyrannise over you—and this to a man of your temperament is one slow and certain way of 'running down.'

There is a grave ethical side of this worldly common-sense which I have been inflicting on you. As a man falls into habitual slackness of body and brain, his soul sinks into 'a state of moral lassitude and collapse.' Whereas the patience and perseverance of the saints shine brightest in that fortitude which sets itself steadily to make the very best possible out of every hour in every day. The best possible in your case will not seldom be golf, or music, or sleep, to ensure a still better day to-morrow. No man has any right to live below his proper level, or to fritter his highest self away. Least of all dare a minister suffer himself to be handicapped in his duty because he ignores the simple hygiene which is observed by a prize-fighter, or neglects the elementary self-discipline in trifles which is required in a telegraph clerk. Forgive me if I have written as though I were not persuaded better things of you. I might be less concerned if you had fewer gifts to squander and spoil. But you will never do justice to your vocation until you have learnt to husband your own health and energy and time. We must mix an ounce of serpent to our pound of dove.—Yours most faithfully, OMICRON.

XIII

To a Minister troubled by the Intellectual Disparities in his Congregation

To a Minister Troubled by the Intellectual Disparities in his Congregation

MY DEAR SIR,—Your Monday morning letter is brief, but it really makes one feel as uncomfortable as the changes between screech and wail in an exceptionally dissonant steam siren. Did Councillor Butterman snore during the sermon on Sunday morning? or the young persons in the milliners' pew pass notes to each other and put on the airs of kittens? or was it the domestic servant in full view of the pulpit who was looking out answers to questions propounded in the Bible-class? Again you are bewailing the mental disparities in your hearers, and speaking contemptuously of their confusing demands for absolutely incompatible types of pulpit work. You are still haunted by the left-handed compliment of the platelayer who said to you, 'When I got home from service, sir, last night, my wife asked me, How did you like the sermon? and I said (now, sir, you must not be puffed up), Well, better. It was more practical.' It is a real trouble to you that you have not the art of winning people of all classes, for you are ambitious to earn the verdict passed on the Master's preaching, 'The common people heard Him gladly.' Again you are expressing the wish for a congregation where the principle of intellectual selection has been at work for a generation, and you recoil from heterogeneous assemblies of men and women who in birth, education, natural capacity, self-culture, are a medley. Perhaps you have changed your pastorates too often, and have been lacking in the patience which allows time for some measure of reciprocal assimilation to take place between preacher and people.

That your congregation, looked at from the political standpoint, is composite, partly clay and partly iron, is one of your minor troubles. You have the good sense to abstain from touching those questions on which it is conceivable Christian men may think differently, although on Temperance, Peace, and Social Reform Sundays, your trumpet gives no uncertain sound. You have sometimes thought your Conservative hearers have been a trifle shy, till the memory of the fierce fulminations of these special days has been softened by time; but you can bear that. Now and again you are disconcerted when two or three Unitarians of the suburbs, who are at a distance from their own place of worship drop in on wet Sundays, and you half wish they would stay away. You are a little confused in prayer, and do not feel quite sure your phraseology will fit in with their theological shortcomings. If the sermon affirms any specific principle of Trinitarianism, you are half tempted to manipulate the awkward dogma into rose-flushed and magniloquent metaphysic. You have sometimes resolved you will never take a strictly evangelical subject on a wet Sunday, lest it should be looked upon as an affront to the creed of unorthodox visitors. Social disparities in your congregation give you occasional trouble and perplexity. In face of apparent evidence, you have sometimes to try and convince the poor that the rich seat-holders are not so cold and supercilious as is commonly supposed, and you have to convince the rich that they ought to speak to their humbler fellow-worshippers without introductions. And in spite of all you do it seems impossible to make the church a large home circle.

The trouble, however, which looms darkest in your soul, is that the congregation is such a promiscuous concourse intellectually considered. Your church has had the misfortune to undergo frequent changes in the pastorate, and the men who have succeeded each other have belonged to widely different types. The metaphysician, the special missioner, the anecdotalist, the premillenarian, and the rhetorician have each created little knots of admirers. And to this disadvantage there is added the fact that you are in a slowly filling suburb, and receive temporary or permanent adherents from orthodox and nondescript churches of the city, and all the variations of the city ecclesiasticisms seem to be epitomised in the people who come to you for lodgings and possibly a home. You could name not a few whose intelligence seems to be overshadowed by their piety, and a few with whom the case is reversed, whose piety seems to stand in a subordinate relation to the reason and imagination. You have a sprinking of hearers who find their Paradise in a Browning, a Shelley, or a Ruskin Society, and more than a sprinkling who look upon the 'abundant entrance,' as attendance at a mission-room dominated by a fervent but more or less crude Plymouthism. You say that you are not equally well fitted to each section of the congregation, although you have not quite lost your early versatility. If time and strength and public opinion would allow of it, you would like to treat your congregation as though it were a big school, and parcel it out into classes, dealing in turn with the children, the domestic servants, the working men, students and professional men, and the young ladies who read stories in the lighter magazines and have taste without strong intelligence. That would be your scheme if you were a benevolent autocrat and could make people obey. When you address the half of the congregation you most respect, and with which you are in closest mental sympathy, many of the others are listless, and it needs a whole week of careful and almost effusive pastoral attention to counteract the centrifugal influence of one of your best logical or expository sermons. You are often tempted to feel how content you would be in your present sphere if you could shed the less cultivated section of your hearers and replace them by thinkers after your own heart.

Are you not in danger of classifying your people by social tests and standards? In the abstract you are a conscientious believer in the principle of equality, and whatever the working men and women of your congregation may think of your preaching, they speak of your homeliness and familiarity with the warmest gratitude. But when you have been mortified by some trifling symptom of inappreciation, you always underline the fact that these uninterested hearers belong to the humble strata in your congregation. Of course it was a pair of domestic servants, or at best dressmakers, who were overheard commenting unfavourably upon your sermon as the congregation was retiring the other night. It was the greengrocer, not the smart medical student, who

THE CLERICAL LIFE

folded his arms for a nap as soon as the text was given out a fortnight ago. It was not the mistress of the High School and her assistants who were interchanging notes in the pew, but shop-girls. Left-handed compliments about the sermon come from unskilled labourers, and not from hard-headed artisans.

You are perhaps scarcely alive to the fact, but your abstract principle of equality is in serious peril. Some of your well-to-do people tried to capture you for their set, and to indoctrinate you with disdain for the set just below it. They have not yet made you a snob, but do not put down all inappreciation to the poor and half-educated, and find your way into the pitfall of snobbery by some other pathway. You know perfectly well that domestic servants in your congregation would, in some instances, pass a better examination upon the topography of the Pentateuch or the argument of the Romans than their well-dressed mistresses, and that the son of the patron Crœsus of the Church has read less since he left the University, than the first half-dozen artisans whose names come into your memory, and that the best essay of the season at your Literary Society was given by a dressmaker. To group your hearers like a public school into six forms may possibly be an ideal method of instructing men and women of unequal mental capacities, but never assume that the social status is any criterion of receptivity. And moreover, I beg leave to think that you would destroy the brotherhood of the church if it were possible to carry out your fine scheme.

This ideal of a congregation of picked hearers, however grateful to the idiosyncrasy of the preacher, would make the Christianity of the Church a dispersive rather than a uniting power, not to speak of its utter impracticability in rural districts and small towns. You have to vindicate a place in the church not only for the poor, but for the slow-witted and unread, and you have to vindicate it by saying something which will capture their attention and retain their interest, even though your thoughtful people should assert you are falling away a little. It will not do to tell the men and women of slow, heavy temperaments that they can get the style of preaching they are craving for at the mission-room, and that they had better go, or to remotely hint it to them even by silently ignoring their special requirements in your ministrations. The fact that some modern congregations have been formed upon a principle of superfine selection is partly responsible for the absence of working men from our churches, and the drift of a remnant who have the savour of piety about them to mission-halls. You could interest these people if you were humbly and patiently to apply yourself to the task, for your early power of adaptation has not entirely died away. The crux of the difficulty is that you are unduly sensitive to the judgments of your more intellectual hearers. What comment will they pass upon this popular performance? You are ashamed not of the Master Himself, but of the rudeness and illiteracy of some of His sincere followers, and you dare not address them on the level of their elementary ideas. A quiet curtain lecture usually rewards these self-sacrificing efforts, and the superfine say, 'The minister was not quite himself to-day.' You dare not imperil your reputation with the select few. Some of these crude and ungifted souls are stung, not so much by the superciliousness of the man in the gold ring and gay apparel, who says, 'Sit by my footstool,' but by the fact that the Master's own messenger ignores their needs as they fill the obscure corner to which the pride of the church has consigned them.

Are you not in danger of assuming that the congregation has been made for the minister rather than the minister for the congregation? To a man who revels in the deep truths of God and the art of presenting them, there will always be a temptation to look at things from his own special standpoint. He is inclined to assume that God has put five or six hundred people into the world whose brains have been organised, hearts tempered, and education planned to fit them to respond with prompt fervour to the message of the man who sermonises according to the rigid rule of his own temperament. But this phenomenon of concurrent adaptation is rare. Never forget that you are a servant of the church, and of its dullest and least interesting members for the Lord's sake. You are sent to shepherd the silliest and most empty-headed lambs, and not to feed a penful of prize sheep only tricked out in gala ribbons and tinkling with silver bells. The Master called you to be a pastor full of His own indulgent largeheartedness, and not the fastidious proprietor of an ecclesiastical raree-show. You crave general appreciation, not, I am sure, in the spirit of personal vanity, but as a sign that your ministry is quickening thought and leaving its mark on the people. It is, of course, pleasant to have knots of refined and effusive devotees around you, but your vocation is wider and nobler than that. Sometimes it may be that your hearers affect to be uninterested in your homilies, for the simple reason that the conscience has been stoutly smitten, and the operation is not altogether agreeable. If you are to say right and wholesome and saving things, you must pass, like the Great Teacher, through epochs of depression and unpopularity. You cannot always be on the crest of the wave, and at the same time cross the unregenerate inclinations of some of your hearers. Bear it, and do not be tempted to make the truth vague, edgeless, saccharine. Men will sometimes forgive the truth that is spoken if it is couched in a witticism or suffused through an epigram, but it is a question then if the truth really reaches them, for they retain the phrase for its own sake, and let its essence pass into oblivion. Church and preacher do not exist for intellectual ends.

I am not sure it would be good for you personally to have a congregation formed by a process of strict intellectual selection. The Christian law of sacrifice must sometimes assert itself in the brain, and the religious thinker is just as much in danger of becoming a Sybarite as the purple-robed gourmand. The principle that 'he that loseth his life for My sake shall find it,' is true for the man who aspires after scholarship and literary culture. If you had the opportunity of addressing only picked hearers, you would find that the task would narrow the range of your thought and expression. Men may get into the habit of thinking in one register of the intellect only, just as some speakers drone away in one register of the voice, and the effect in both cases is equally strident and unedifying. One or two of your more conspicuous gifts are in danger of riding rough-shod over their neighbours, and unless you can find the providential antidote, your sermons will become monotonous, philosophical generalisations, spiced with the catchwords of modern literature. You need colour, contrast, variety, briskness, and you will get these qualities by giving a thought now and again to the less intellectual section of your congregation, and settling down into a sympathy with their modes of thought and phraseology innocent of all patronage. All subjects do not admit of a severe intellectual treatment, and you will have to miss much out from the presentation of Christian truth if you are governed by extreme literary ideas.

It is not always by high intellectual methods that intellectual men are the most profoundly influenced. You have examples in your own church of those with whom, times without number, you have discussed the difficulties of faith for hours together, and for years they seemed as incapable of moving towards definite goals of faith as though the fate of Lot's wife had overtaken them. But an itinerant evangelist with unction, fervour, common sense, and little formal logic came by, and they received a surprising spiritual impetus. Or business reverses and family bereavements befell them, and you feared the surviving fragment of faith would be lost; but strange to say, the imperilled faith rebuilt itself from the very foundations under the shadow of a soul-racking mystery, and your laboured and ingenious apologetics seemed to count for little more than the wisdom of this world in God's inscrutable economies.

I have spoken plainly, almost truculently. Forgive me. You have drifted into a morbid, miserable mood, and need to be well dosed with quinine and iron.—Believe me, yours sincerely,

THETA.

XIV

To a Minister who has Studied in Germany

TO A MINISTER WHO HAS STUDIED IN GERMANY

DEAR MR. BAXTER,—We are all heartily sorry that you have decided to leave us in October. The church at Plymouth has a smaller membership than ours; the salary, we understand, is much the same, and there are two troublesome deacons. The call was hardly unanimous, and the only possible explanation of your acceptance is that you are running away from Herr Diekirch.

Three years ago you came to us with a considerable reputation for learning. You were without a University degree, but it was understood that the degree of Ph.D. would shortly be conferred upon you by a German University. You explained that your course at the Theological College was cut short owing to your earnest desire to study abroad. The Principal and Professors, we gathered, had regretfully decided that it would be selfish to keep a young man of your ability in England. Every one who hears you preach takes away some pleasant reminiscence of your student life at Bonn. It was a pity, perhaps, that your funds only held out for six months; but certainly, no young man ever bought up opportunity more eagerly. 'To say that these six months gave a colour to my after life would ridiculously understate their influence. They have saturated my inmost consciousness. I might almost say, without exaggeration, that I think and dream in German.' So you wrote in your preface to *Translations from Heine and Uhland*, which were printed at the *Chronicle* office in our High Street. The deacons were naturally proud to have secured a minister who thought and dreamt in German.

In your first sermon, you delighted us all with the remark, 'I once discussed this text with the learned Professor Hammelfleisch, of Bonn, and he thoroughly upheld the exegesis I have given you.' Several of us looked about the chapel in hopes that representatives might be present from the Baptist Church round the corner. Their

THE CLERICAL LIFE

minister is a B.A. of London, but we have never heard that he thinks or dreams in any language but his own.

Interesting references to fellow-students frequently occur in your preaching. A brilliant assembly of geniuses must have gathered at Bonn in your year. Your acquaintance with scholars is nearly as extensive as Whang the Miller's with rich folk. If a vicar is appointed to a canonry, if a dissenting minister is advanced to a professorship, if a writer makes a sudden reputation, we shall hear next Sunday that Mr. So-and-So was a friend and fellow-student of your own. 'His promotion does not surprise me,' you will add ; ' he was a man who made his mark even in the learned and exclusive circles of a foreign university.' It was gratifying to know (also from pulpit allusions) that you kept up an active correspondence with some of the foremost scholars of Germany. Half the children in the congregation were beggars for your foreign postage-stamps. Soon after you came, I called at our bookseller's for a few sheets of thin writing paper. He said he had sold the last to you, and that you purchased six quires at a time. The incident naturally made a considerable impression on my mind. For some time we believed there was a conspiracy among the German Universities as to which should offer you a professorship. Old Dr. Annesley, who presided at your recognition service, told us we had chosen a very remarkable man, a man who would make a European reputation.

My first visit to your study was a memorable occasion. You have few books, but nearly all are German. The floor was littered with German newspapers and pamphlets. The air felt heavy with wisdom. Our former minister had a collection of English sermons in which he took great pride. But, in presence of your library, I felt ashamed of his ignorance. Portraits of living German writers adorned one wall, and on another were prominent historical and literary personages from the same country. A certificate of merit, dating from your time at Bonn, was framed in gilt, and hung above the mantelpiece.

We had the gratification, as a church, of knowing that your stay in Germany had done you no harm. Whatever anxiety we may have felt on this score was dispelled by Dr. Annesley. 'Mr. Baxter,' he said, 'is a learned man, and he is also a safe man—a combination almost unprecedented in these dangerous times.' Not unfrequently you have gone out of your way to warn us against the Higher Criticism. 'Although I myself enjoyed peculiar opportunities for studying the Higher Criticism at its fountain-head, I kept myself resolutely aloof from the temptation. My dear master, Professor Hammelfleisch, attracted me from the beginning by his noble orthodoxy. Surely the history, literature, and politics of Germany afford a sufficient field of study, without our needing to wander in the dark and devious by-ways of criticism!'

After a time, strange as it may seem, some of our members grew weary of Germany. It was a proof, as you truly said, that we are not an intellectual people. Minds in our town are sluggish; the circle of interests narrow. I myself was never tired of a subject so instructive and fertile, and I could not understand why the young men of our Debating Society took exception to the lecture you kindly offered us last winter. The title was 'Past and Present of the German People.' The year before you had given us 'Glimpses of Life in the Fatherland.' In your first winter the subject was 'Rambles by the Rhine,'—in my opinion a most delightful and refreshing travel paper. The true reason why so many objected to 'Past and Present' was that your long course of week-night lectures on 'The Saints and Reformers of Germany' had somewhat fatigued their attention. Still, even when most weary, the congregation was proud of your attainments. We looked on you as a great national authority, the Livingstone of an undiscovered country. When you started a German Reading Circle, and presented the members with second-hand German primers, your fame as a linguist reached its zenith. 'Every one,' you said, 'can learn German, and every one ought to learn it. I wish the young to join my circle; but the middle-aged and the elderly should join it too. Every man, woman, and child in the congregation may, with perseverance, become a perfect German Scholar.' You achieved the great triumph of enrolling as a member Mr. Simmons, our wholesale grocer, who had never been known to read anything but the *Weekly Chronicle* and the *Grocer's World*. None of us were very eager to learn, but we enjoyed spending an evening in your study, watching the grave, spectacled faces on the walls, and wondering how much German would be needed to make us look so wise. We reproached ourselves for the trouble we gave you with our accent, but, somehow, the tongue of our countryside does not fit itself easily to 'vons' and 'zus.' We glanced at the correspondence on your desk, and seeing envelopes addressed to 'Herr Professor' this, and 'Herr Doctor' that, we wondered why the Ph.D. was still withheld. Sometimes you visited London, and then we imagined you were called into consultation with scholars at the British Museum. We pictured you dining with foreign publishers or exchanging student memories with distinguished authors from Berlin.

All would have gone on well if Herr Diekirch had not come to the town. When he became German master at the Grammar School, and afterwards a member of our congregation, we flattered ourselves that a friend worthy of you had at last been found. But somehow, you and he did not draw together. At the Reading Circle you appealed to him anxiously on every trifling question. We resented this, for, after all, he was an ordinary German, while you were a scholar and a future Ph.D. Still, at first, we saw no harm in Herr Diekirch. His mild blue eyes looked as if they had never known malice; his smile was kindly, and his manner slow and humble. But not long after his arrival reports began to creep about the church. It was whispered that your accent was bad, that your sentences were ungrammatical, and your translations frequently erroneous. One after another the members of the Reading Circle dropped off. 'I am tired of this German,' Mr. Simmons said to me. 'I've been neglectin' business lately, and customers don't like it. Besides, they say the minister does not understand the language over well himself.' Some such whisper must have reached your ears, for a striking change took place in your preaching. For four successive Sundays Bonn was never mentioned, and Professor Hammelfleisch seemed to have faded out of memory. Then the call from Plymouth came; in spite of our persuasion, you accepted it, and already you are packing up your books and photographs. Herr Diekirch has driven you away from us.

I shall come to hear you at Plymouth, and shall expect some reference to Bonn and Hammelfleisch. But take my advice and don't weary your congregation. People are not anxious to know much about Germany. We have a sincere admiration for your ability, but we shall choose as our next pastor a man who thinks and dreams in English.
—Yours, X.

XV
To a Divinity Student

M

To a Divinity Student

DEAR ANDREW,—Your aunt and I are sorry that the preaching engagement you have undertaken for the coming winter will prevent you from making our house your home. We had hoped to keep you with us until you were settled in a church. Since the change must be made, I take this opportunity of expressing the gratitude of two old people for the sunshine you have brought into their lives during the four years of your divinity course. We are plain, simple folk, and must often have appeared slow and dull to a young man with five bursaries and an honours degree. But your constant kindness and affection have endeared you to our hearts, and for your companions also we have a warm regard. Perhaps you and they will pardon me if I touch for a moment on one or two points that have puzzled us.

When you entered the Divinity Hall, we had no idea that the principal and professors were such an incompetent set of men as we now understand them to be. Their names were familiar to us in the pages of newspapers and from the proceedings of Church Courts. Your aunt derived great benefit from a study of Professor Murchison's *Lectures on Hebrews*, and Principal Grant White's *Meditations for Morning and Evening* has for years been a favourite devotional book of my own. Professor Douglas draws a crowd whenever he preaches, and you would be the last to deny that Professor Shiel's scientific researches have an international celebrity. At first I was disposed to envy your good fortune in sitting at the feet of such men, but now I quite see, from all you have told me, that they have been sadly overrated. The wonder is that a great Church like ours, full as it doubtless is of genius, learning, and judgment, should have bestowed its highest posts on men who are so obviously unfitted to fill them. Many times we have listened with painful interest while you and your friends have discussed the 'dulness' of 'poor old Murchison,' the 'verbosity' of the learned principal, the 'claptrap sermons' of Dr. Douglas, and the 'crude theories' of Professor Shiel. Your talk, like Vivian's, seemed at last to leave

'Not even Lancelot brave, nor Galahad clean.'

We were sorry that the rising generation of theologians should have fallen upon such evil times. It is greatly to the credit of yourself and your companions that you should have achieved such excellent results under circumstances so discouraging.

If there is one professor who has the affection of the Church at large, it is Dr. Mitford Ellis. His stirring missionary sermons, his long experience in the foreign field, and above all his saintly character, have won him universal admiration. I am told that he is not popular at the Hall, because his method of teaching is antiquated. It is surely a grave mistake on the part of the Church to allow any one who is at all antiquated or out of date to have a part in the training of its young men. Your aunt and I agree that a reform of the professorial staff is urgently demanded, and should immediately be taken in hand.

Most of the professors are exceedingly kind in asking students to their houses, but even their hospitality has been made a ground of complaint. 'Murchison and the rest of them ask everybody without discrimination,' a friend of yours remarked one evening. 'Their invitations are so cheap that it is hardly worth one's while to accept them. They ought to restrict themselves, as the University professors do, to a few of the best men.' Scraps of conversation such as these have convinced me that professors should not be too genial.

Your criticism of ministers would strike me as severe if I had not welcome evidence of the ability of our students, who are certainly destined to revolutionise the pulpit. Preaching, you have often told us, is at a miserably low level; and though we, in our old-fashioned way, still delight in Dr. Newington's sermons, modelled, as they are, on Dr. Chalmers', we admit that Dr. Newington does not attract the young. On the other hand, since you are not here to argue with me, I will venture to repeat that I infinitely prefer his discourses to that dry, monotonous sermon preached from our pulpit last winter by your idol, the Rev. Patrick Spens. 'Uncle Walter,' you said, when I ventured to hint my disapproval of the Rev. Patrick, 'do you know that Mr. Spens is universally admitted to be the ablest man in the Church, and that there is every likelihood that he will be called to St. Augustine's as colleague and successor? I am afraid a long course of Dr. Newington has spoiled your taste in preaching.' Quite possible, my dear boy, but I am glad that your style, however hard you may have tried to model it on that of Mr. Spens, still retains its fresh colour and its warmth of imagination and feeling.

When you are a 'placed minister'—and a young man of your talent will not be kept long waiting—you will know how to avoid all the faults which you so heavily and so justly condemn in others. You will never be guilty of the crime of preaching an old sermon. You will never waste on golf the precious hours that should be given to pulpit preparation. Tennis matches and afternoon tea-parties will not lure you from the path of duty. Every sermon of yours will show the very latest results of English and foreign scholarship. Closely as you study, no one will ever accuse you of neglecting pastoral visitation. You will also find time to write a number of useful works on theological subjects. You will take a prominent part in reviving the Liberal party in your neighbourhood, and will exemplify your own maxim that a good preacher must also be a good public man. It is a real satisfaction to your aunt and to myself to remember that we are only just turned sixty, and may hope to enjoy your triumphs.

To touch for a moment on a different topic; it has long been in my mind to thank you for the valuable literary counsel and help I have received from you and your fellow-students. It is rare and delightful to find young men with opinions so divided and judgments so matured. I have never known any of you hesitate for a moment in pronouncing on a book. The whole

THE CLERICAL LIFE 185

range of ancient and modern literature has been passed in review by your keen and searching intellects. You are perhaps rather too ready to assume that other people have read nothing. 'Why don't you read Byron, Aunt Agnes?' I heard you say one evening, when your aunt was quietly perusing Mrs. Browning. 'Mr. Spens believes we are on the eve of a great Byronic revival, and I agree with him. How is it we have no copy of Byron in the house? Can it be possible that neither you nor uncle ever read him?'

Your aunt went to the bureau where she keeps her wedding presents, and brought out a delicately bound Byron which had not lain there quite undisturbed through all these years. She was not in the least offended because you thought *her* ignorant, but she took it to heart that you should have said to Dr. Newington, 'I suppose, sir, you have never made any special study of the Lake School?' Dr. Newington's *Memorials of Wordsworth and Coleridge* passed through three editions in the early forties.

Why is it that you and your classmates so greatly object to quotations from the pulpit?

Business men are not able to read so much as they would like, and it is refreshing to hear pretty verses, which have long slipped from one's memory, brought up again in a sermon. The youngest school of preachers makes a merit of being very dry and stiff, concealing emotion and setting every subject in the cold light of reason. Take my word for it, nine out of ten church members like a quotation and enjoy an anecdote. Last winter you and I went to St. Augustine's to hear the great Principal Franks of Cambridge. I came away enraptured. Such a sermon I had never heard since Dr. Guthrie died. 'Good enough,' was your verdict. 'But this is the third time I have heard him quote from *Obermann*.' Depend upon it, the great preacher knew better than you or I how to catch the attention of his hearers.

We have noticed with pleasure that you and your companions have a very high opinion of each other. Professor Shiel has no microscope half so powerful as that under which you see your comrades' gifts and virtues. I suppose there never was a time when our Church was so poor in teaching ability and so rich in brilliant learners. M—— seemed a very ordinary young man when he spent his first evening in our house, but we know now that he took the prize for elocution in his second year. R—— has written an essay on the Reformation which called forth warm praise from Principal Grant White. (In spite of the painful inferiority of the professors, you are all very ready to quote their compliments.) C—— made his mark in the debating society, and G—— construes Hebrew almost *more* correctly than the learned principal. It would be impossible to exaggerate the satisfaction with which your aunt and I have seen so many brilliant young men at our table. Dr. Newington listens to your talk with a smile and a sigh, and says you remind him of the 'Woman of Three Cows' in Mangan's ballad :—

'O think of Donnel of the ships, the chief whom nothing daunted—
See how he fell in distant Spain, unchronicled, unchanted!
He sleeps, the great O'Sullivan, where thunder cannot rouse—
Then ask yourself, should *you* be proud, good Woman of Three Cows?'

Dr. Newington recalls his own contemporaries, his 'Donnel of the ships' and his 'great O'Sullivan,' and he cannot admit that all the genius and glory of the Church has been centred on the last four years.

Long ago, when your aunt and I were young and had our way to make in the world, we took a divinity student as a boarder. His many excellent qualities were obscured by what seemed to us his insufferable conceit. After he left college we lost sight of him, and when we next met, he had been a probationer for three years, and a settled minister for five. He had developed into one of the kindest, most humble, and most charitable of men. The experience of real life had cured him of his superficial faults, and had brought out the real gold of his character. In your case, my dear Andrew, there is happily no need for such a lengthened process. At heart you are modest and self-distrustful, and in a very short time you will refuse to believe that you ever carried about with you the 'air' of the divinity hall.—Your affectionate uncle,

X.

XVI

To a Martyr of Procrastinating and Pessimistic Moods in Sermonising

TO A MARTYR OF PROCRASTINATING AND PESSIMISTIC MOODS IN SERMONISING

MY DEAR FRIEND,—For many reasons I wish you could correct those unhappy habits about which we talked at my last visit to the Manse, and of which your letter again reminds me. I remember your wife joined in with allusions to the click of the type-writer long after Saturday midnight, and the pacing to and fro, in the intervals of composition, on the study floor just over the heads of sleeping babes. Her raillery was pleasant and light-hearted enough, but I could not help suspecting that she thought these late hours in the study a family nuisance, which would be stopped if the codes of the household were as strict as those of the municipality. Perhaps this in itself is not a very strong reason why you should become a reformed character, because, after all, the arrangements of a minister's household, no less than those of a business man's, must sometimes give way to the exigencies of public work. Nor do I attach very much importance to what may be said on the ground of health, for to a man of average constitution it does not matter much when he gets his sleep so that he does get it in due proportion some time; and you rightly and wisely allow yourself a complete holiday on Monday. The strong arguments for amended methods are that you are constantly accusing yourself of wasting time in the week, and feel a dissatisfaction with the meagreness of your achievements that almost amounts to a malady; your hurry when close upon the sacred responsibilities of pulpit work is so great that you have scarcely time for a due cultivation of the devotional spirit; and your present method of mooning drearily over your Sunday subjects for two or three days, and then doing everything with a gigantic spurt, is apt to make the latter half of the week black, bilious, fevered, unbelieving, when it ought to be full of bright anticipations of the power of the Word. From neither the intellectual nor the religious standpoint is it well for you to do your work under the spur of an overstrained Saturday night, for reaction is sure to come, and the reaction, as you have already confessed, sometimes begins before you have got through your very important Sunday evening service. If you are to have true mastery over yourself, and get the maximum result out of the powers God has given you, you must reduce your moods to a more perfect order.

I allow that something may be said in excuse for your late start. Till the business committees, which come in the early part of the week, and the outside engagements, which perhaps ought not to be undertaken, and the week-night prayer-meeting, which practically means a short homily demanding a morning in its preparation, are over, you do not feel yourself free to come to a decision about your Sunday work. I confess that I myself share your repugnance to the methods of some worthy men who map out a whole year's subjects for their congregations in the course of their summer holiday. I have not a little sympathy with the view held by those estimable people the Quakers, that we should speak under direct intimations given to us from above, and I cannot imagine that the wise and holy Guide of the Church and its ministers would crowd the brain and heart of any man with intimations of what he must do in the course of a twelvemonth's ministry. For my own part, I do not care to be tied up by having subjects announced beforehand either from the pulpit or in the press. It gives me a sense of uncomfortable restraint, and I can never be sure that the subject will fit in with the special thoughts and feelings which may be dominating me at the time. It is sheer wretchedness to have to preach on one subject when thought and interest and sympathy happen to be rallying round some other. You, like myself, are unable to keep two or three subjects under consideration at the same time, for it is inconsistent with concentration of intense thought and feeling upon any one of them. You want, before you can settle your texts, a free and a quiet hour of thought; and when the organist sends mid-week for your hymns, which must have a more or less direct adaptation to the texts, his messenger often seems like an emissary of Satan come to buffet you. The fresher a subject is to your mind, the greater your ease in preaching it; and perhaps the best thing that can be said for your present method is, that inasmuch as you can no longer memorise a subject after the method of your College days, the fever of high-pressure preparation burns a subject into the brain and heart, and makes it easier of delivery than a more deliberately prepared subject.

The question, 'What shall I preach? wherewith shall I feed this people?' often haunts you as painfully as the unbelieving question of the over-anxious business man, 'What shall we eat, and what shall we drink, and wherewithal shall we be clothed?' It is your practice to keep a list of subjects which in the course of your devotional reading have suggested themselves as profitable topics of study, and picking out the topic around which thoughts have begun to crystallise, or perhaps, fixing upon one that has more recently suggested itself, you propose for once to make an early beginning. At the first glance you seem to have in hand a subject which admits of interesting treatment, and one, too, of which your congregation may be very profitably reminded. But a few days or weeks ago there were lights upon it which seem to have vanished, or emotions were quickened by it which will not revisit you, however eagerly you woo them. You cannot see your way into the subject. The glamour of interest is gone. It does not leap up like some men's sermons into hot, copious, inexhaustible geyser springs all at once. The ground over which you had prospected seems to have become dry, barren, unpromising. You hover round the subject for two or three days, and nothing in the way of a sketch has suggested itself which it is worth while putting on paper. Rightly or wrongly, you then begin to reproach yourself with an enormous waste of time, and yet you are posing before your people as a busy man. You are going to fail, and the patience of your people will be tried, and what little reputation you have lowered, for the subject will not open out, and your first view of it is proving a mere mirage. You jib and shy like a nervous horse, and wish you had chosen some other topic.

THE CLERICAL LIFE

The first watch of the Saturday night finds you in the deepest gloom, and turning wistfully to piles of old papers, and wondering whether you cannot trim one of your college rockets and let it off again. But as you glance at the gay and highly decorated crudities of your youth, your heart sickens more and more, and you rightly resolve it will be better to stammer out a few sober truisms than bring yourself to that humiliating pass. You groan and moan, and invite your merry little wife to share your forecasts of pulpit tribulation. Twelve o'clock comes on apace, and you let down your literary ideal of what a sermon should be, and under the weird compulsion of midnight hours, put down whatever comes first. Like the Indian conjuror, you make the mango-tree to grow in an incredibly short time, and happily your tree has upon it fruit which to some at least is refreshing. The subject does prove interesting and profitable, your tribulations were more or less visionary, and whilst you ran a risk of failure by allowing yourself to drift to the very last moment, you did not entirely fail.

Now is it not possible for you, even though your methods are hardening into habits, to get the upper hand of these moods, which make you so unhappy, and to all appearance waste time which might be devoted to profitable reading? We once talked together about that fine sermon of Martineau's on 'The Tides of the Spirit,' and agreed that the work in which the highest powers of the mind are to take part cannot be done by rule of thumb. Our noblest thoughts come to us unsought and at intervals. Perhaps you can do a little of the rumination which must necessarily precede actual sermonising as you go upon your pastoral rounds or take country walks. If the account you give of yourself is perfectly correct, you do seem to fritter away time before the sermon-making actually begins, and you must not allow even sermon-making to narrow the range of your reading, or your mind will become like an impoverished and infertile soil, and production will be an increasingly difficult and burdensome task for you.

Is it necessary that everything you say should have the stamp of the uncommon and the superfine upon it? You have marked literary tastes which you have diligently cultivated, but those tastes are apt to become a temptation to you. I am sure you are perfectly sincere in your faith, and always preach from the depth of genuine conviction, and I entirely sympathise with you in your desire to keep out of old ruts. But it seems to me that you are in danger of finding subjects attractive because of the speculations to which they allure, or the literary form with which it is possible to clothe them, and of looking upon some subjects as vapid if they must needs be treated upon old lines, however stern and solemn the facts with which they deal. Remember, my dear fellow, that there is such a thing as intellectual selfishness, and that it is quite possible for a man to become a pulpit epicure. Cannot you feel an interest in some phases of the truth because of their practical fitness to those whom you address, whether those phases of the truth lend themselves to philosophical, parabolic, or picturesque treatment or not? Your power of dealing with abstruse forms of truth is invaluable, but it must be compensated by practical sympathy with the needs of the common people. Perhaps this weekly ordeal of dulness, disheartenment, heart-sickness, pessimism, followed by a rush of preparation and delivery like that of the scorcher cyclist on the race track, is due in part to intellectual fastidiousness which must be cured by closer contact with all classes of life in your congregation. When God means you to preach only to the members of the Athenæum Club, He will give the shareholders a dividend which will allow them to engage a chaplain.

The languor and despondency which sometimes trouble you during the construction of a sermon may arise in part from the sense you have of the inadequacy of human language and of all poor earthly metaphor to limn the mere outlines of heavenly things. You have gifts which do not often go together — imagination, the power of abstract thought, and a deep fund of spiritual emotion — and you sometimes see the things of God with very little apparent help from speech. I think I have heard you say more than once that you could disprove out of many of your own intellectual experiences the dictum of Max Müller, that language came before thought, and that we cannot think without language. High thoughts very often come to you before language, and when you have to put them down in black and white it is very much like trying to put a farmer's rough driving-coat round the form of an angel. When you are sickened by feeling the paucity and limitation of human language, read a little of something at once rare and simple in phrase by way of correcting this pessimism, and be careful to choose something as far away as possible from the line of your ordinary reading. It will revive your faith in the possibilities of expression, and make you feel in a moment they are larger than you had thought. And keep the instrument in perpetual tune. The mind must rest now and again. Your hearers will be the better through the temperate recreation you allow yourself, and the little excursions into social life you make now and again. But watch over yourself, and keep from settling down, even for a few days only, into the groove of an unproductive mood.

If your thoughts will not take wing, turn to some stimulating book for an hour, but a book of such a quality that you cannot take in too much at a time. Never gorge yourself like a literary Red Indian. Read just enough of a poet to warm your sensibilities out of their torpor. And if possible, make it a rule to break into your subject as soon as possible. It is true you may not be breaking into it at the right point, but it will be a saving of time if in the end even you have entirely to rearrange it. It is an advantage to get into a subject whether you get at it by the main gateway or not, for you will be able to reach the centre in due time by whatever pathway you advance. But these, after all, are counsels of minor importance, and perhaps scarcely need to be written.

 I am an old friend, and will use the privilege of my position and speak plainly. Let me ask you to probe your own motives as deeply as possible, which I am sure are mainly right. Do not these pessimistic and procrastinating humours, which are fast settling down into a chronic malady, imply a more or less defective consecration to God and your work? Some faint strain of ambition may enter into the conception of your task, and debar you from counting to the fullest possible extent upon Divine help. You have come to think that the popularity you have achieved with the thinking and reading sections of your congregation is an essential constituent of your usefulness, and are a little fearful lest the ebb tide should set in. Let God give or withhold public favour as He may decree, but it is a dangerous thing for you to aim, in however subordinate degree, at keeping it. Be anxious only about your usefulness, and God will take care of your popularity, if He thinks it good for you and His work that it should still attend your ministrations. You are sometimes perplexed by this lower aim which asserts itself in your subconsciousness. I know your supreme aim is to teach the truth and commend yourself to God; but this subordinate aim seems to intrude itself into your study like Poe's Raven, and the desire to please God on the one hand, and be acceptable to the choicest spirits of your congregation on the other, exerts quite a paralysing influence upon your productive faculties. Think of yourself as Christ's bond-slave, as did St. Paul, and remember that to be a bond-slave is not only to be more absolutely subject to the will of your master in the methods of your work than is the hired labourer, but is also to have a claim upon his help and support not possessed by the hired labourer, who only serves within prescribed lines.

You once knew yourself to be Divinely called to the ministry of the Word, although the routine of the last ten years has sometimes brought you almost to the verge of perfunctory automatism. And you feel this fact still standing as a solid thing in the background of your pessimistic vapourings and trepidations, although the atmosphere of hurry in which you live for much of the week prevents you from being adequately impressed by it. When you sit down to your next sermon, remember the subject has been prayerfully and conscientiously chosen, and do not hark back from it in some dyspeptic or hysterical mood which is unworthy of you. Have just as much faith in the providential suitability of your subject when you begin, and the beginning seems unpromising, as when you came down the pulpit steps last Sunday morning, thanking God that the thing had turned out so much better than you expected. Try and have a little faith during the days of preparation as well as in the act of delivery. Never allow yourself to be mastered by the temptation that it will be better to turn to something else, or that the subject may prove so tame and colourless that you will be compelled to show contempt for your own offspring by presenting it to the congregation in a humdrum, passionless, semi-apologetic tone. True, you may not have those gifts of voice and action, and shall I add of superficiality, which enable some fortunate men to turn platitudes into entrancing music; but there is no reason why you should allow yourself to drift into the style of the politician who is said to have yawned in the middle of one of his speeches, and have said afterwards to some friends who reminded him of the lapse, But was it not frightfully dull? Do not let these vapours visit you either in the study or the pulpit. If they come into the study, you will find that they will want to follow you to church as persistently as the shepherd's collie. It is true your tastes are fastidious and exacting, but you must be as lenient to yourself as to your brother minister's criticism, of whose pulpit efforts I am glad to find you never fail to temper with magnanimous kindness. Your sermon now and again may not count for much as a study in theology or an effort in literature, but as a practical counsel to the living men and women for whose spiritual welfare you are set to care it may be of a value that can only be told in the arithmetic of the judgment day. If some mysterious hand seems to put to sleep for a while those faculties of the mind which make you coruscate, believe that your Master for once in a way has something better for you to do than to be brilliant. Never be solicitous about your effectiveness in the intellectual sense. The art of captivating the men and women to whose intelligence and culture you perhaps pay rather too much homage for your own comfort, will be continued to you if it will contribute to your all-round usefulness. Never forget 'the Lord has much people' in sections of the community which lack appreciation of those purely intellectual qualities about which you are so anxious in the throes and agonies of the weekend.

I am sure you will forgive the freedom of my letter, which perhaps almost verges on the inquisitorial; and if you can correct the malady about which I have been writing, you will be a happier and a more effective man, and will thank me for my plain speaking in after years.

With every good wish for you in your work, I am, yours affectionately, THETA.

XVII

To a Minister who objects to 'Wandering' in August

O

To a Minister who objects to 'Wandering' in August

DEAR MR. ARMITAGE,—Last Sunday evening, for the second time since I joined your congregation, you gave out as your text, 'As a bird that wandereth from her nest, so is the man that wandereth from his place.' You were to start on Monday morning for a six weeks' holiday in Norway. I was to spend August at my desk in Moorgate Street. Past experience had made me distrustful of the 'supplies' you were likely to provide during your absence, and I had secretly resolved to hear a few of the eminent strangers who are at present occupying our London pulpits. But the steady direction of your eyes towards my pew, coupled with sundry hints I have lately received from you, made me certain that I was the 'wandering bird' you were anxious to retain in the nest.

As one of your young men, I am naturally proud of your growing reputation. I seldom turn over the pages of a religious newspaper without finding some mention of your name. It is even whispered that you send paragraphs about our church and its pastor to most of the daily and weekly journals. Far be it from me to find fault with you for this. To my mind it is part of a very wise and skilful policy. How are we to bring our work before the notice of the Christian public if our pastor yields to a foolish and ill-advised modesty with regard to himself? Such a paragraph as the following, which I cut out of a paper this week, may not at first sight appear to be of absorbing national interest : ' The Rev. R. Hamilton Armitage preached on Sunday morning to a crowded congregation from Micah iv. 1. In the evening Mr. Armitage gave an address to young men from 1 Tim. iv. 8.' I agree with you, however, that every reader of this paragraph will want to know what you said on Micah iv. 1 and on 1 Tim. iv. 8, and will look out with eager interest for any further mention of your name. Some of your brethren have accused you of self-advertisement, but if your people appreciate these paragraphs you can afford to be indifferent to envious outsiders. I feel a new pride in my Church, my minister, and even my suburb, when I read that 'The Rev. R. Hamilton Armitage, in his eloquent sermon on "Charity," dwelt with convincing force on the thought that kind hearts are more than coronets.' At the same time, I cannot accuse myself of 'treacherous disloyalty' because during these few autumn weeks I venture now and then to wander. 'During my absence on a much-needed holiday,' you remarked on Sunday, 'I shall expect all the members who remain in London to be regular in their attendance at public worship in this place. I was grieved to learn on my return last year that there had been a sad falling-off in numbers and in contributions. The young men especially had been conspicuous by their absence. To all those who neglect their own sanctuary and roam idly abroad to other places, the solemn warning of the text applies, "As a bird that wandereth from her nest, so is the man that wandereth from his place."'

But what if the bird never wandered from

its nest? Would its life be fuller, richer, stronger because it brooded continually within those narrow walls? And has not the bird the right to ask that its nest shall not be made too uncomfortable to hold it? This brings me to the chief remonstrance of my letter, which I offer with the utmost humility and deference. Why are the 'supplies' you provide for us in August, as a rule, such wretched failures?

One of your young men has a theory that you search the length and breadth of England for the worst preachers our denomination can produce. You have a preference for very old men whose powers of utterance are failing. Last summer not one of our holiday supplies was under seventy. We had a sermon on 'The Evils of the Higher Criticism,' and another on 'The probable course of the Ark before and after its arrival on Mount Ararat.' Deacon Mulgrave, who makes a boast that he has not slept out of his own house for twenty-eight years, nor worshipped in any 'strange sanctuary' (your favourite phrase) during the whole of that time, was intensely interested in both of these sermons, but especially the latter, as he said it opened up a new world, and made one feel like a friend and companion of Noah. There are plenty of Deacon Mulgraves in our congregation, and you might surely allow the rest of us a little freedom. After all, we young men pay a high compliment to your preaching by refusing to listen to any one else in your pulpit. I can quite understand that you like strangers to see a crowded area and galleries, even at this holiday season, a visible sign of the invisible energy which binds us together. But you need not be anxious on the score of personal reputation. There were two rows in the gallery vacant on the third Sunday of last August, and Mr. Mulgrave went into the vestry to make a formal apology. 'It has never happened before,' he said. 'A vacant seat is unknown in our church. We have a room downstairs full of chairs and benches for placing in the aisles, and when Mr. Armitage is at home every chair and every bench is needed. Hundreds are turned away during the winter. It is only a few of the young men who like to wander during August.'

So, you see, our empty seats increase your

honour and prestige, and the poor old 'supply' wonders why he has never, in his long ministry, been able to draw together more than seventy hearers. *Why* is it, I wonder, that you give us such inferior preachers for the holidays? One of the older members told me lately that you engaged, some ten years ago, a very distinguished man who is now the principal of one of our colleges. The congregation were enraptured, and for a whole week nothing was heard but comparisons between his style and your own. 'If we could get a man like that,' said the grumblers; and even your faithful friends wished you could take a lesson from the stranger. You were amazed on your return at the effusive gratitude with which every one spoke of Dr. S.'s sermons. He has never been asked back to our chapel. Yet surely you, who have nothing to fear from a rival, need not have taken fright so hastily.

It is a pity, I think, that you are so hard on American preachers. 'If you must wander from the nest,' you said, 'at least don't let the love of mere sensation take you to popular orators from the other side of the Atlantic. American preaching is shallow, trivial, pretentious, and unedifying.' After this I decided to hear a few of the eminent Americans who are in London during the summer, and I only wish you had secured an American instead of one of our usual group of fossils. To a business man like myself there is something eminently welcome in the plain and business-like tone of those American preachers. 'Some of my younger hearers,' said a noted D.D. from New York whom I heard the other day, ' have been, no doubt, on the switchback railway, and will appreciate the application I propose to make from its workings to this part of my subject.' The awestruck and reverent interest with which American preachers refer to material wealth and rank is also very gratifying to a City man. Even our humdrum old Deacon Mulgrave would prick up his ears if his minister, leaning over the pulpit, announced with earnest emphasis, 'I heard an anecdote lately, dear brethren, about a great English duke, a man of vast wealth and consequence, perhaps the richest of all Queen Victoria's subjects.' London audiences like to hear Americans during the summer. For some of us it is the next best thing to crossing the Atlantic. Engage Dr. Hiram Winnipeg of Chicago, and I guarantee we shall be satisfied to remain.

If, on the other hand, you think it right to give village pastors an opportunity of preaching in London during the summer, do not grumble too much if we younger folk slip off. Strangers are sure, at this season, to be found in sufficient numbers to fill our vacant places. Even in the great churches of London the congregations during August are largely composed of visitors; and although the minister may himself be at home, a certain freedom is required during these summer months. We may be chained to the desk on week-days, but we give up our evenings to the river or to games with twice the enthusiasm of any other period of the year. We are at work while the world is on holiday, and so we try on week-day and Sunday alike to find as much holiday as possible in our work. The bird is forbidden to fly into the free fields of heaven; why should you forbid it to flutter a few feet from the nest? After all, the mind needs freshening—never more than in a London August. If the great preachers are content to see a scattering, and never dream of asking whether the Jenkinses are really in the country, or if they have gone to hear the eloquent American over the way, why need you be so stringent?

Depend upon it, we shall welcome you back none the less cordially because we, like you, have wandered. The familiar walls will be more home-like because we have worshipped for a time with strangers. We shall open the old hymn-books with a sigh of relief, because we have handled others marked 'For Visitors Only.' The great man from Chicago is on his homeward voyage, and most cheerfully we have sped the parting guest. The bird that wanders farthest flies back to its home.—Yours very truly,

X.

XVIII

To a Brother smarting under a Bad Time

To a Brother Smarting Under a Bad Time

MY DEAR SIR,—When I met you in the train yesterday, I was sorry to find you so wofully depressed about the specially bad time you seem to have had in your pulpit last Sunday. Your failure is evidently worrying you, and a few lines from an old hand may prove not altogether unacceptable. I have suffered too often and too deeply from the same cause to be now indifferent to your perplexity and wretchedness. The times are very rare indeed in which the preacher is altogether satisfied with his deliverance; usually he is conscious of falling sadly below his ideal; but ever and anon the cleverest and most successful pulpit master is conscious of miserable failure. The preacher's distress on these occasions may be little more than a matter of wounded vanity, but I know you well enough to be sure that more than personal considerations enter into your grief. It is true that to accentuate your chagrin the distinguished Dr. Twigem was present in your congregation to witness your confusion, and you will find the famous critic always does drop in on these melancholy occasions, yet I am persuaded that no mere personal considerations constitute the sting of this unlucky incident in your ministerial life. It is the general feeling of incompetence that these occasions generate; the loss of confidence in ourselves that they involve; the sense of a fine opportunity wasted; the belief that through our awkwardness and blundering we have lost caste in the eyes of our people, and can no longer address them with the same confidence,—these are the more worthy and serious sources of a faithful preacher's humiliation. The sorrow that springs out of a thoroughly bad time is often almost tragically keen, and it need not be altogether ignoble.

Let me remind you that strange and unaccountable failure is common to all intellectual workers. Tennyson showed more than once that the poet is not always in his singing robes.

Leech confessed that sometimes his pencil was on strike, that it was a dangerous anarchist, and that he proposed to call out the military. The lips of the orator are not always touched with fire. Napoleon said of Waterloo: 'It was a day of fatalities,' and all intellectual agents are familiar with such days. Regarded simply as a brain-worker, the preacher must expect to share in these eclipses and collapses. There are days in which we are not ourselves, in which we are guilty of inexplicable lapses of memory, obvious inconsequence in reasoning, absurd confusion of metaphor; we cannot quote correctly the familiar verses, we get hold of everything at the wrong end, or by the wrong handle. Some failures admit of ready explanation, they are the obvious result of hurry, illness, disturbance, but the obscure cause of many a pulpit muddle and martyrdom must be sought in this curious mental inaction and infelicity.

You will remember also that the more free a man's style of working is, the more liable is he to these occasional embarrassments. The more mechanical the artist's method, the less likely is he to sudden, ignominious failure. Now you have adopted the extemporaneous style of preaching, and I am glad that you have; on the whole I believe it to be the far better course, but you must be prepared to pay the penalty of such a style. The preacher who elects to read his sermons knows comparatively little of bad times, as, indeed, he knows comparatively little of times of extraordinary inspiration and triumph: the extempore preacher knows both. Victor Hugo says: 'An ass with his chart is better off than a wizard with his oracle,' and all extemporaneous orators have times when they prove the truth of this aphorism to the sorrow of their soul. Knowing on the one hand the advantage and pleasure of free, spontaneous speech, you must not, on the other hand, shirk the penalty of your choice in occasional failure and humiliation. When you trust to your wings you cease to stand upon your feet.

The intellectual part of the failure, however, is often with the preacher the least part of the bitter experience. The more grievous defect in the miscarriage is the lack of spiritual reality and power. The preacher has no vivid sympathy with what he is talking about; the words come constrainedly aud coldly, but the truth does not move his soul, light his eye, tremble on his lip. There is spiritual deadness as well as mental constriction, and the hour that ought to be so rich and blessed is barren and disappointing. How far your calamity of Sunday evening was an intellectual or a spiritual limitation, or both, no one knows so well as yourself.

So far as you are personally concerned, this pulpit paralysis has its special lessons which you must not disregard. Not rarely our bad times are the consequences of inadequate preparation. My dear friend, I am more and more shocked at the little attention which some give to pulpit fitness. Other intellectual workers bestow infinite pains that they may attain perfection in their particular vocation, whilst the preacher too often presumes on the slenderest special effort; and all the time no branch of art calls for more intense endeavour than the sermon does. James Smetham says of Leslie: 'On the floor of one of his pictures there are about half a dozen small flowers scattered. It is recorded that for these flowers there are sheets on sheets of studies in water-colours of flowers from nature.' Yet some of our brethren think to dash off a sermon in the most light-hearted fashion. Every work of merit represents concentration; every true worker is a passionate worker; and men will hardly continue to do things badly if their heart is in the doing of them. Nothing should reconcile a minister to superficial and hasty preparation for the desk, and if failure ever follow on such preparation it should prove a caution. Then if the preacher has done his best to prepare the discourse, he has not always the consciousness that he has done his best to prepare himself; he has wrought his best in the study, but has not been living at his best. The actor entering on the stage has no special reason to look into his soul; the state of the imagination, not of the conscience, is the primal solicitude of the painter; the musician taking up the score is concerned only about his voice; but the moral and spiritual elements in his own heart and life are of transcendent interest to the preacher whenever he stands forth to address his people. The best work of the pulpit can be done only whilst a spiritual and divine enthusiasm agitates the preacher's own soul. Our failures ought to cut us to the quick when we have neglected brain or heart. I would not, you know, speak with levity of those affecting moments when we give the final touches to our personal appearance before mounting the pulpit, the coaxing of the tie, the disposition of the locks, the adjustment of the gown, the farewell pathetic glance at ourselves in the vestry looking-glass—these are delicate things only to be witnessed by a deacon's eye; but if such trimmings constitute the main part of our pulpit preparation, the sooner we break down finally the better for all concerned. I know you are a good and diligent fellow, but we all need to watch against spells of sloth, and to preach to ourselves more faithfully than we preach to anybody else. In case our heart does not condemn us, either for intellectual or moral default, then we may take our bad times with graceful resignation. Our moods of humiliation are not our most dangerous moods. The days of brilliant triumph are the days when our feet are set in slippery places. How beautifully you cheered your deacon the other day when he made that bad debt; administer similar consolation to yourself, smarting under a bad time. This is the discipline that persuades us what we are; which afresh teaches us humility and dependence; which illustrates once more the commonplace that we have this treasure in earthen vessels, that the excellency of the power may be of God and not of us.

Our congregations are less affected by some of these bad times than we suppose. We are ashamed to meet our people on Monday morning, we would turn a corner to miss them, we are afraid that they will learn to despise us. But much of this is a mistake. A stranger like Dr. Twigem, dropping rarely into our church, might easily put us too low or too high, but our own people know our best and our worst, and, on the whole, judge us fairly. They know the average, and their estimate of us is not greatly affected by a specially glorious or inglorious day.

Nay, putting aside all cynicism, is it not a fact that all of us are estimated rather by our best than by our worst? The great masters are remembered by their most splendid achievements, only antiquaries recall their failures; cricketers are known by their big scores, authors by their 'hits,' painters by the pictures which were railed round to keep off the crowd at the Academy exhibition. Orators are immortal by a single speech if it only were of signal excellence. And, depend upon it, my young friend, the preacher shares in this generosity of the public judgment. A congregation familiar with a minister's earnest words and works will not forsake him because occasionally he falls below himself. Our people simply smile whilst we are foolishly sick at heart.

It is often easy to exaggerate the significance of our bad times. They will not exactly arrest the progress of Christ's kingdom in the world. Contemptible speech' very early wrought marvellous things in the Christian Church, and it has vindicated itself a thousand times since then. It is wonderful how many failures on the part of its advocates the Gospel has survived. He who works with poor human instruments does not see such a great gulf between our best and worst as we see. He who can use us at all can use our blunders and confusions. It is a failure indeed in which no true seed is sown; in which no helpful words are spoken. Andrew Bonar writes to Mr. Milne of Perth: 'Only get above the clouds, brother. We must think only of how the Lord may be glorified. . . Never mind vigour or want of vigour, comfort or want of comfort, in our preaching and ministry. All we have to do is to do our best as we get strength at the time, and, as Robert M'Cheyne used to say, "The Lord can show us how to catch fish with a broken net." "Be of good cheer." Our works do not save us, our ill-success will not destroy us.' Lay these words to heart; be a vessel meet for the Master's use; and none of your words shall fall to the ground.—Affectionately yours, BARNABAS.

XIX

To a Minister who has warned his People against 'Intellectual Preaching'

To a Minister who has Warned his People against 'Intellectual Preaching'

DEAR MR. DOVEDALE,—At our social meeting on Wednesday evening we listened to an earnest address from you on the snares of intellectual preaching. This is a subject to which you frequently return, and you have often reproached us with the example of your former congregation, who 'expected no swelling words of man's wisdom, but were content with the simple proclamation of the Gospel.' We, as a city church, are in your opinion peculiarly exposed to the temptation of exalting the intellect. But congregations in all parts of the country are demanding more and more from their ministers, until the danger is, as you express it, 'that the house of God should become a mere hotbed of culture.'

'There are certain things,' you told us on Wednesday evening, 'which no church has a right to expect from its pastor. I am not here to minister to your mental gratification. The Apostles themselves refused to follow "cunningly devised fables," by which in our day they would have understood the greater part of modern literature, especially the vast portion which comes under the head of novels. Yet there are preachers not a few who, turning away from the Scriptures, seek their own spiritual nourishment and the nourishment of their people from novels and even from newspapers. I grieve to make such assertions against my brethren, but the instances are many, and the people love to have it so. Then, again, it is expected that the preacher shall encroach upon the sphere of the politician and devise remedies for social evils. He is required to keep himself abreast of the periodical literature of the day—a task before which the boldest might shrink, and one which a Christian congregation has no right to impose. I tell you frankly that when I stand at a railway bookstall and see the multitude of newspapers, magazines, and reviews which lie spread out as tempting baits before the public eye, I am haunted by the sad change which this flood of ephemeral literature betokens in our modern life. In my boyhood we read a newspaper once a week, and a single magazine supplied us with abundant interest for a month. We read little, but we meditated much. Now I go into your homes, and I see the *Nineteenth Century* and the *Contemporary* and the *Fortnightly* lying on your tables, and you are astonished that I have not mastered the contents of these reviews. Even on the day of publication I have been asked by my younger members whether I have read such and such an article from the magazines. I have even detected a shade of supercilious scorn in your faces when I have answered that my time is too valuable to be wasted with such trifles. Dear friends, I am not ashamed to inform you that I have a hearty contempt for modern journalism in all its branches. It has lowered the life of the nation and impoverished the life of the Church. Where do we now find that patient study of the Scriptures which was the business and delight of our ancestors? The newspaper is mastered at the breakfast table, instead of being kept, as it ought to be, as a recreation for the tired brain when the work of the day is over. I have reason to believe that many of my young men spend no inconsiderable sum on evening papers. While I would not of course venture to dictate to them, I may be pardoned for suggesting that the money thus wasted might with far greater benefit be devoted to helping the schemes of the Church.

'In any case,' you proceeded, 'my people must not expect me to bury myself under a drift of penny and halfpenny newspapers. A venerable friend asked me last week what I thought of Cardinal Vaughan's reply to Mr. Birrell. I was not aware what he referred to, but I answered that our own denomination provides so many points of interest that I do not observe minutely what the Roman Catholics are doing. This is merely one specimen of the troublesome and annoying inquiries to which I am continually exposed.'

Next you went on to deal with the request of the young men's Bible Class that you would give a series of evening sermons on Dr. ——'s great work on Modern Theology. 'I have refused this request for various reasons, each of which is in itself sufficient. For one thing, I have not read the work in question, and have not leisure to undertake so formidable a task. Profound theological study is no more necessary for a preacher than the daily study of the newspapers. He has to minister to the poor and needy, and his words must therefore be the plainest, simplest he can find. I am sorry that my congregation expect deep doctrine and abstruse thinking from this pulpit, because it is beyond my power to gratify them. A further reason why I have refused to preach on this book is that I wish to discourage young men from poring over theological and critical works. These books, even when written, as they sometimes are, by devout and earnest men, have a bad effect on young minds. They raise doubts which but for them would never have troubled the clear sky of faith. I would suggest that the young men of this church should read less, and give more attention to the musical part of our worship. The choir greatly needs reinforcement, and our choirmaster will be glad to receive the names of helpers. Many of you, I am sure, would be wise to devote a little time to gymnastics in the evening. If you must read, choose first the greatest authors. Do not study Tennyson till you have mastered Shakespeare. Follow the example of the man who said that when a new book was published he read an old one. Above all, do not forget the wise saying of Solomon that " much study is a weariness of the flesh," showing clearly that in his opinion life was given us for nobler purposes than reading.'

As a corollary to your speech on Wednesday, we have the address you delivered at the autumn gathering of the Union, on 'What Congregations may reasonably expect from their Pastors.' If I remember rightly, you drew up a very interesting list of ministerial duties. Especially you dwelt on the importance of visiting. It was your privilege to minister to one of the most cultured and intelligent congregations in London, and though it was no easy matter to keep up to the level of their intellectual requirements, still they were inclined to pardon much in a minister who neglected his study for the work of pastoral visitation. Half an hour's pleasant chat had a better and more lasting effect than the weightiest and most learned discourse. 'It is useless to deny, brethren,' you went on, 'that many of us middle-aged ministers have small Latin, less Greek, and no Hebrew. Our college days lie far behind us, and we should be puzzled, I imagine, if we were asked to construe a page of Virgil or Sophocles. Are we for that reason less valuable or less efficient workers? I say we are more valuable and more efficient, and many passages from the New Testament might be quoted in support of my contention. "Not the wisdom of this world" is a motto which might well be inscribed over every pastor's writing-table. The less we are burdened with earthly learning, the more we shall be thrown back for our inspiration upon the Scriptures. Take, for example, our relations to the Higher Criticism. I have told my people frankly that in this matter I should observe an attitude of the strictest neutrality. I should neither condemn the Higher Criticism nor defend it, and in order to escape temptation, I have refrained from any examination of critical writings. "The empty traveller," as the old proverb has it, " can laugh in the robber's face," and the man who declines to fill his brain with the air-woven speculations of the critics has nothing to fear from their assaults. There is truth, as well as humour, in the suggestion that we should look a difficulty fairly in the face and pass on, but, for my part, I would have my brethren pass on without looking.'

I have quoted at some length from these two speeches, both of which I had the pleasure of hearing, in order that, if I have misapprehended your meaning on any point, you might have an opportunity of correcting me. In reply, I would first point out your mistake in supposing that we are a specially cultured and intellectual people. We are an ordinary congregation, made up largely of business men, who have received an average education and who read neither more nor less than the ordinary middle-class Londoner. In the next place, it is a great mistake to imagine that either we or any other congregation that I know of expect intellectual preaching. We may look back wistfully to the great men whom we remember in our boyhood, or of whom our fathers have told us. We may wonder how it is that these men have left few successors. Sometimes we may regret that our children will not have such opportunities as we enjoyed. But we expect very little nowadays. Thirty years ago there were in the London pulpit at least twenty men whose sermons might have taken the rank of classics. They were not confined to one or two denominations, but were found in the Church of England and in all the Nonconformist bodies. We take down their volumes from our shelves, and wonder whether the genius of the pulpit has died utterly away. A few still remain with us, but the walls of their churches cannot be widened to contain the whole of London. Are there any others coming up behind them? How many among the younger men will exert as wide an influence?

To my mind, the most remarkable sign of the times is that congregations are willing to be satisfied with so little. The education of the general community is far ahead of what it was in my boyhood, but preachers are making no effort to keep abreast of the wider knowledge of their people. Suppose that all the sermons preached in London on any particular Sunday could be reported and submitted to a competent judge, how many would he select as fit for print? The laity, it seems to me, are very generous to ministers. They know that many sermons are feeble, but they consider the heavy burden of outside work that falls upon the pastor, and judge his preaching leniently. It seems a little hard that the men for whom we are making these allowances should warn us with such solemn emphasis against the perils and snares which beset the lover of intellectual preaching.   X.

XX

To a Minister who inclines to Condescension

To a Minister who inclines to Condescension

DEAR MR. SUNDERLAND,—In the time of your predecessor, Dr. Vernon, our congregation was in danger of holding too high an opinion of itself. Dr. Vernon liked to flatter us with such phrases as this : ' I can never forget that I am addressing one of the most cultured and intelligent congregations in England.' Dr. Vernon invariably assumed that his people had read the books that he had read, and were in all respects his intellectual equals. During the two years of your ministry amongst us, you have done much to rectify this mistake.

You take it for granted that we have little or no knowledge of the Bible, or of Eastern customs. ' Many of my hearers must wonder,' you remarked some weeks ago, ' when they hear of conversations taking place and of business being transacted on the roofs of houses. How was this possible? you inquire, remembering the sloping slated roofs to which we are accustomed in England. We are apt to forget that in the East all the roofs are flat, and that they were used for much of the most important business of the household.'

You explained to us in full detail how it was that the labourers in the market-place could hire themselves for so low a sum as a penny a day. 'Even the poorest man who now listens to me would rate his services higher than this; in fact, we all know that under present conditions human life could not be supported on so low a sum. But a flood of light falls on the passage when we remember that a Roman denarius or penny was equal to $7\frac{1}{2}$d. of our coinage, and also that money in New Testament times had a much higher value than it has with us.' In a sermon on the good Samaritan, you expounded with much care the puzzling verse about 'pouring in oil and wine.' 'Many of my hearers, no doubt, imagine that the oil and wine were both poured into the wounds of the unfortunate traveller; but a moment's consideration will show you that this would only tend to aggravate his sufferings. The oil was poured into his wounds, and the wine into his mouth.' Dealing with the same parable, you informed us that roads in Palestine were very different from the highroads of England. They were infested with robbers, and even in modern times many travellers had perished on the road between Jerusalem and Jericho. You delight in explaining such expressions as 'a shoe's latchet,' just as if none of us had ever attended Sunday-school. 'The Orientals, dear friends, do not wear boots or shoes, but on account of their hot climate, are content with sandals. The latchet of the sandal must not therefore be confounded with the ordinary boot-lace.' 'Witness-bearing among the Jews' was the subject of one of your most instructive sermons, but you need not have assumed that every one in the congregation believed that the ancient Hebrews had trial by jury. In a course of lectures on the wilderness journey of the Israelites, we came to the verse, 'a land flowing with milk and honey.' 'To many of my hearers these words must present insuperable difficulties. How can a land be said to flow with milk and honey?' But the difficulty vanishes when we remember that the Old Testament writers frequently used the language of hyperbole —a long word, brethren, but it means a figure of speech which involves exaggeration—and in this glowing sentence the ancient chronicler means to set before us a land of vast wealth and of boundless fertility.'

'The Murmurings of the Israelites' was the theme of a recent discourse, and you remarked that an English congregation could with difficulty understand why the Hebrews in the desert were always clamouring for water. 'In our damp and rainy climate we cannot even imagine the sufferings of travellers in these arid, sandy regions, where the parched soil yields not a drop of water, and where the deceitful mirage lures the wanderer to his doom.'

'The decree of Cæsar Augustus, that all the world should be taxed,' furnished a noble subject for your explanatory genius. 'Those of my hearers who are themselves taxpayers must frequently in reading this verse have reflected on the vast revenue which the taxing of the whole world must have brought into the coffers of Augustus. You will be astonished when I tell you that this "taxing" was not a payment of money, but merely the taking of a census—in simple words, a numbering of the people—a process to which we ourselves are accustomed every tenth year.'

Every one must appreciate your anxiety that we should make no mistake as to the meaning of Scriptural language. Not many months ago you chose as your text, 'If any man speak, let him speak as the oracles of God.' 'I have no doubt, friends, that the word "oracles" awakes misgivings in the minds of many of you. The thoughts of my more cultured hearers will be carried back to Delphi or Dodona, to the voice of the priestess of Apollo, or the whisperings of the god through the leaves of the mulberry trees. Even those who know little of classical mythology may feel that the word "oracles" has a remote and pagan meaning. Let me therefore explain exactly what the Apostle had in his mind when he used this expression.'

Shall we ever forget how laboriously you explained the meaning of the word "Selah," when it occurred in your first exposition of a

Psalm? 'It may have struck the more attentive Bible students among you that there are not a few Hebrew words scattered up and down the Old Testament. One of these is "Selah." It signifies "a solemn pause"—perhaps a rest between two bars of music. When it occurs in the reading of a Psalm at family worship, do not say the word aloud, but make a longer pause than usual before passing on to the following verse.'

It was scarcely surprising that we should not know why treasures were found in the fields of Palestine, when the most careful searcher would fail to find them in England. But you might, I think, have assumed that we knew that Eastern shepherds went before their flocks. I could multiply without end examples of your condescending habit in the elucidation of Scripture, but this is by no means the only department in which our ignorance distresses you.

At the Mutual Improvement Society last winter you gave a series of 'very simple' lectures on Evolution. Most ministers, you told us, were content to leave this thorny question alone, but

THE CLERICAL LIFE

you preferred that the young men of your congregation should not remain entirely ignorant of the march of science. I must apologise for quoting the opening sentences of your first lecture as given in the local paper of that week, for they are an excellent specimen of your general method. 'The word Evolution is to many of you a hard, a dubious, and a meaningless word. You connect it in some vague manner with the names of Darwin, of Huxley, of Tyndall, but if you were asked for a definition, you would be hopelessly nonplussed. I want you, therefore, to write down in your notebooks that "evolution" comes from the Latin *e*, out of, and *volvo*, I roll, and that it means a gradual rolling out, unfolding or progression of things from a lower to a higher plane.' Mr. Hilditch, who is one of the most active members of the Society, and a B.Sc. of London University, attended the first of the lectures, but he told me he would not be able to find time for the remainder of the course.

Our congregation is much interested in foreign missions, and it was an excellent innovation on your part to give a missionary sermon once a month. Many of the members have, however, been annoyed because you found it necessary to name the exact locality of every mission station. It is not only that you point out such places as Pekin and Calcutta on the map behind the platform, but you take it for granted that we have heard of very few places outside the British Islands. 'How many of my hearers, I wonder, could put their fingers on the Fiji Islands, one of the most hopeful of mission fields?' 'The great river Congo flows westward like the Niger, and, like the Niger, loses itself in the Atlantic Ocean.'

In everything that concerns modern literature you take it for granted that we are sunk in a depth of ignorance which no Fiji Islander could surpass. You never quote the simplest phrase from Tennyson without remarking that 'some of the congregation may recognise those lines as the work of the great Laureate who was recently taken from us.' We appreciate the kind interest you have always shown in our reading, but is it necessary to assume that we must start from the very foundation? 'Milton is a poet little read nowadays; perhaps I may conjecture that not five persons in this congregation have ever reached the end of *Paradise Lost.*' 'It is an amazing fact that hardly any one nowadays seems to read Sir Walter Scott.' For this winter you have planned a series of 'Elementary Browning Studies,' and we are all looking forward with interest to the first lecture, on 'The Pied Piper of Hamelin.'

In justice I must admit that there are certain subjects on which you concede to us a full and ample knowledge. Women are supposed to be experts in all that concerns the household, and men to have an accurate knowledge of the drudgery of business. These are matters on which you sit at our feet, as we must sit at yours in all that concerns a liberal education. I was present at your address to the mothers' meeting last Friday, and was interested to see that you had no domestic advice to give them. 'Dear sisters, you know much better than I where the home burden presses. You know what it is to rise early and sit up late, and to eat the bread of carefulness. You have experienced the toil and struggle which it costs to keep the house sweet and beautiful, and to have the meals ready against your husband's return. You need no counsel and no instruction as to your household duties.' Then you proceeded to advise the working men's wives not to waste their time on stories brought home by their children from the Sunday-school library, but to nourish their minds on the great English classics. The business men in the church rather resent your assumption that they are minutely acquainted with the shady side of London commerce. If ever there is a financial crash in the City, you take the opportunity of assuring us that we must know many scoundrels quite as bad as those who are now detected. Apart from disagreeable hints of this kind, we feel that you need not be so pathetic in your descriptions of our City life. Old Mr. Arnold, who received a clock from the Sunday-school on the occasion of his business jubilee, was quite cross because of the pitying tone in which you described his life. 'Have you ever thought, children, what sacrifices a man like Mr. Arnold must have made, in order to be punctual morning after morning in the city during fifty years? In rain and snow, in storm and sunshine, he has had to shoulder his daily burden and go forth with the vast army of toilers. Mr. Arnold could tell us much about the sorrows, the disappointments, the trials of a merchant in the City of London. He has come through anxieties of which we happily know nothing, and has worn throughout them all the white flower of a stainless character.' Mr. Arnold, a stout, prosperous, merry old gentleman, who inherited a splendid business, and who has got home comfortably at five o'clock every evening during the last forty years, showed a very natural reluctance to accept these compliments.

I wish to say in conclusion that we cordially appreciate your many excellent gifts, and that we fully understand that your habit of condescension will disappear as you grow older. The members of your church will love you all the better when you learn to treat them as equals.   X.

www.ingramcontent.com/pod-product-compliance
Lightning Source LLC
Chambersburg PA
CBHW031350230426
43670CB00006B/495